Praise for *Single*

Offers true wisdom, practical advice and laughs too. What more could a person ask for in one book? Every single person should run out and get this.

—M. J. Ryan,
author of *Attitudes of Gratitude* and *The Power of Patience*

At last! A kind and funny book for uppity women who revel in the single life—and for those who fear it. In *Single*, Judy Ford reveals the bright side of the singles coin, and shows others how to live it with grace, style, and joy. In today's society, where all of us stand a good chance of being single, married, and divorced in our lifetimes, Ford's advice fills a real need. As she says, 'Being single is often the best choice. It's as natural as being together, and you'll probably have a go-around at both.' Three cheers for this frank guide to the art of single independence.

—Vicki León, author of the *Uppity Women in History* series

Single is about upholding the most enduring relationship of all; the one we have with ourselves. Yes! When you know yourself you are never lonely, even when alone. Read and learn how to relate to your true self.

—Bernie Siegel, M.D.,
author of *365 Prescriptions for the Soul* and *Help Me to Heal*

Uplifting nugget for those who are single.
—Gerald G. Jampolsky, author of *Love Is Letting Go of Fear*

Imagine a woman in love with her own life. A woman satisfied, fulfilled, and independent. Judy Ford reminds us that everything we need and want is right here, right now. Through her words we fall in love, again, with our own messy, ordinary, sacred lives. We don't feel so alone after reading Judy's book.

—Patricia Lynn Reilly, author of
Imagine a Woman in Love with Herself and *I Promise Myself*

single

The Art of Being Satisfied, Fulfilled, and Independent

Judy Ford

ADAMS MEDIA
AVON, MASSACHUSETTS

*To the wonderfully wise, funny, kooky characters
who've been there for me and have lifted me up!*

Published by
Adams Media, an F+W Publications Company
57 Littlefield Street, Avon, MA 02322. U.S.A.
www.adamsmedia.com

ISBN 10: 1-59337-154-3
ISBN 13: 978-1-59337-154-8
Printed in the United States of America.

J I H

Library of Congress Cataloging-in-Publication Data
Ford, Judy
Single / Judy Ford.
p.   cm.
ISBN 1-59337-154-3
1. Single people--Attitudes. 2. Single people--Life skill guides. 3. Single people--Psychology. 4.
Single people--Conduct of life. I. Title.
HQ800.F67   2004
646.7'0086'52--dc22   2004002027

This publication is designed to provide accurate and authoritative information with regard to the
subject matter covered. It is sold with the understanding that the publisher is not engaged in ren-
dering legal, accounting, or other professional advice. If legal advice or other expert assistance is
required, the services of a competent professional person should be sought.

> —From a *Declaration of Principles* jointly adopted by a Committee of the
> American Bar Association and a Committee of Publishers and Associations

Many of the designations used by manufacturers and sellers to distinguish their products are
claimed as trademarks. Where those designations appear in this book and Adams Media was
aware of a trademark claim, the designations have been printed with initial capital letters.

Photographs on pages 53 and 91 © Thinkstock
Photographs on pages 1, 165 and 197 © image100
Photograph on page 129 © Image Source

*This book is available at quantity discounts for bulk purchases.
For information, call 1-800-289-0963.*

Contents

Acknowledgments

You are never given a wish without also being given
the power to make it come true. You may have to
work for it, however.

—RICHARD BACH

Many thanks to Ame Beanland for designing a top-notch pro-
posal that boosted my idea off the launching pad. To literary
agent Jenny Bent for finding a perfect match for me with Adams
Media. To my ever-optimistic and enthusiastic editor, Danielle
Chiotti, for instantly seeing the potential and for her clear guidance. To Virginia Beck and Laura MacLaughlin for adding the
final polish. To Frank Rivera for designing a fabulous cover. A
lifetime of thank-yous to Gethen Bassett, who not only asks
how's it going, but cares about the answer. To Jay Schlechter for
ideas when I had none and whose sweet candor is always an
unexpected blessing. To Linda Seelbach and her team of vibrant
role models, Cathy Houser, Rosie Dorn, and Roz Montgomery.
To Andrea Hurst, for believing in the message of this book. To
Barbara Deede, for unfailing support and spreading my books
around town. To all the singles who so willingly shared their
struggles and triumphs with me. And to my lovely, lively
daughter Amanda Ford for her uplifting spirit and for once again
allowing me to share our story.

Introduction

The Most Enduring Relationship of All

Studies show that dread of public speaking is high on the list of big fears for most people. The mere thought of standing up in front of strangers to deliver a five-minute talk can send spasms of panic through the most accomplished adult. Sweaty palms, racing heart, cold sweats, and stage fright overtake even the most skilled performers. Making a fool of oneself is mortifying, but as humiliating as that might be, I can testify to the fact that the fear of public speaking is a mere tickle in comparison to the seismic ripples of horror that reverberate through the heart when faced with spending a weekend alone. It isn't public speaking, or snakes, or high places that bring adults to their shaky little knees. No, the biggest nightmare of all is the fear of being alone.

No one likes to admit it, but we've all felt it. Spending Friday night without a companion is enough to send folks who don't like the taste of booze running to the bars. Saturday night without a date is the embodiment of the "Something's wrong with me" syndrome. People are more courageous about going to the dentist than they are about eating dinner in restaurant alone. I've suffered from the condition myself. Why, I even walked down the aisle whispering, "Anything is better than nothing."

Yes, millions are terrified of facing singleness. To avoid it we settle for less, hooking up and staying in stale relationships. We marry, divorce, and do it again. It's a vicious little cycle. In desperation, we read books on finding a mate, and when that doesn't work we read books on how to live alone and love it. Sadly, neither approach solves the dilemma because being single is not a condition to be cured. Being single is natural, as natural as being together. One is not better than the other—they are complementary.

Single: The Art of Being Satisfied, Fulfilled, and Independent is a peek into the everyday life of ordinary singles—part memoir, part self-help, part inspiration—the message of *Single* is a clear one. *Single* is about being satisfied and happy as an individual, whether you end up in a relationship or not. Here's the honest scoop about mastering the art. It's worth a try. After all, you are with yourself more than you are with anyone else. Within these pages is the full story—the highs and lows, the love and the anguish. *Single* is a celebration of the most enduring relationship of all—the one with yourself. My hope is that together we can elevate singleness to new heights.

What a Satisfied Single Knows

1. The quintessential ingredient for a great evening is believing that your presence is desired.
2. Life is too short to spend it yearning, looking, and hoping.
3. Friendships with both men and women are essential.
4. Quality is better than quantity. One connected conversation is better than a dozen disconnected chats.

5. Dates with your friend's exes are a no-no.

6. Accepting a dinner date doesn't mean you have jump in the sack.

7. It's liberating to offer to pay your share.

8. An affair with a married person is a lonesome affair and hardly ever worth it.

9. A one-night stand is good for finding out if your equipment still works.

10. It's life-affirming to rise above your heartbreak; it's a downer to whine about it.

11. Never, ever change plans with a friend for a date.

12. Aloneness is a positive feeling of being with yourself.

13. It's a blessing to have a friend who will set you straight when you're getting sidetracked.

14. Creativity is the best antidote to restlessness and boredom.

15. Loneliness is not tragic, awful, or bad.

16. Being kind to yourself when you don't feel like it is the most generous thing to do.

17. It's far better to admit to yourself that you want a lover than to pretend that you don't.

18. It's not okay to lead anyone on.

19. Life has a meaning and purpose that is greater than your marital status, finer than your relationships, bigger than who is sleeping with whom.

20. Words can't describe contentment—it has to be experienced.

21. It's better to have loved and lost than never to have loved at all, and it is better to have loved and lost than never to have lost at all.

22. Going to dinner alone means you're hungry, not that you're a loser.
23. Every interesting man or women has survived a broken heart.
24. If you can't be happy with yourself, you won't be happy with the best.
25. Lonely and alone is preferable to being lonely with someone around.
26. Looking good is pleasurable and always worth the effort.
27. A child needs one parent who thinks that he or she is the best thing since sliced bread.
28. When a friend finds happiness in a relationship, never let jealousy stop you from celebrating with and for them.
29. Every season of singleness has its own delights.
30. The best parties have lots of singles.
31. Flirting is peek-a-boo for adults.
32. Solace and understanding are available when we have the courage to ask for what we need.
33. Friends are people who bring out the best in you and lift you up.
34. Sometimes we want something and we don't want it at the same time.
35. Sharing even the simplest meal is a gastronomical pleasure for both body and soul.
36. Deserting your children for a hot-and-heavy romance is bad parenting.
37. Pouting over holidays, birthdays, and special occasions won't get you anywhere, but planning in advance will.
38. Statistics about singleness are only numbers on paper.

39. Self-respect doesn't have anything to do with anyone else.
40. Your relationship with your child is the number-one relationship.
41. The more relaxed you are about being single, the more at ease you are with others.
42. Self-acceptance is a powerful aphrodisiac.
43. There is always something you can do to improve your situation.
44. Singleness is not fatal.
45. Unrequited love makes you burn with feverish excitement and wears you down. Reciprocal love fills you with joy and makes you soar.
46. Most people wish that more people would approach them more often.
47. There is joy of being known and unknown.
48. It is important to learn how to fall in love without losing yourself.
49. It's possible to break up with a lover without losing a friend.
50. Singlehood is catching on.
51. A lot of people are in relationships who would rather be single.
52. A good catch is a good catch, even though the right one hasn't come along.

1

One
Wonderful
Life

Original Single

Everyone is single. Think about it. We each come into the world as one tiny, little individual. Oh yes, we have a mother and a father, and we may have brothers and sisters and a whole bunch of relatives, but basically each one of us, regardless of our relationship to others, is one human being. We have many types of relationships, which often give us the illusion of not being single at all. Yet if we examine our situation more closely, we see that regardless of our relationship to others, regardless of our marital status, we are still just one little person. Throughout our lives we have playmates and friends, acquaintances, casual contacts, and colleagues. We have lovers and spouses, and various combinations thereof, but still we remain uniquely one human being. No one else ever abides in our skin.

> **We remain uniquely one human being. No one else ever abides in our skin.**

Single Again

For the newly single or recently uncoupled, the adjustment back to singleness is particularly hard. It is the grief that comes with letting go of what's dear, familiar, and loved and heading into the unknown that makes this transition painful. But don't let the grief that comes with going from coupled to single give you the impression that single life is all pain—it's not. When one person is missing, it sometimes seems as if all love is gone. It's missing that one particular person and the coupled touch that's painful, not singleness. Unfortunately, the newly uncoupled, divorced, or widowed often get stuck in shock, fear, and anger. And that's where they remain. Without a road map or mentor, they're unable to make the transition to a wonderful life. When you've been coupled and are single again, it's as if you've been plopped into the middle of a foreign culture. The rules have changed, and everything is unknown. You might not know the language or the customs, but you can learn. And once you conquer the beautiful secrets, you're in for a blessed surprise. A single life is, if you embrace it, filled with incredible magic and meaning.

Single with Relationships

Hooray! Isn't it grand that there are so many lifestyle choices for singles? You can be single and have innumerable relationships from flirting to dating, from friends to living together, from casual to committed. It is beautiful to be alone; it is also beautiful to be with people. Both are complementary, not contradictory; one is not better than the other. No matter what our circumstances, there's both pain and joy. The challenge we've been handed is to be loving, to be friendly, to be forgiving.

A relationship—be it with friend or lover—is a special place. It is a sheltered environment in which we can endlessly explore ourselves in the presence of another and in which we can offer the possibility of the true reflection of another. And still we are one person.

Single, Independent, and Love-Filled

Sometimes we fear that if we are independent and single, there won't be any love. We resist becoming independent because we're afraid that if we do, we'll be lonely, unloved, and uncared for. We suspect that we'll be bored, with nothing to look forward to, and so we resist growing up. That's sad, because we miss out on the exuberance of being in love, in love with life. You see, love is not a relationship. Rather, it's the quality of our own heart. Love is the fragrance of knowing oneself. Love is seeing who you are and sharing your being with others. If you've ever felt like you were in love, but you had no lover, then you know what a tremendous joy an open heart brings. An open heart responds to the goodness in yourself and those you meet. An open heart understands that although you've been through very rough times, you're committed to doing the very best you can. It wants to be open and to experience the fullness of life. Singleness beseeches us to take care of our inner needs, to pay more attention to our center, to love our very own self. Singleness urges us to take exquisite care of our life.

When we look back at our single history, we begin to understand how the single experience is a vital component of who we are. It's this blending of experiences that makes us unique.

Single segments are essential for listening to the call of our soul. If you're in a single segment, you're being called to embrace the blessings, privileges, and lessons of each passage. There's a plan for you in the making, and it's probably bigger than what you can see.

Yikes! I'm Alone!

I'm one person, and I'm alone. Yikes! That reality hit me for the first time when I was ten years old. I don't remember what triggered the realization, but I vividly remember the sudden insight and the cold chills that came with it. I was lying in a sleeping bag in the back yard, looking up at the night sky. There I was, counting shooting stars and constellations, when I was overcome with awareness that I was separate from everyone else. My parents were inside the house entertaining company, my brother was playing next door, and my friends were not around. Wham! It hit me! I was just a lone me in a sleeping bag under a universe of stars. Yikes! I got it! I was me! No one else was me! I was one girl, Judy, in an ocean of others. All through the night as I slid in and out of sleep, it seemed to me that I had discovered a giant secret. Why had no one told me? Was this obvious to everyone else? I wanted to share my epiphany but was afraid to admit that what seemed so obvious had only just dawned on me. And so I pushed my revelation aside.

My breakthrough forgotten, life proceeded in the way that I expected it to go. After high school, I went to college, met the man of my dreams, graduated, got married, and had a career on the side. I was twenty-nine years old when the thunderbolt of singleness hit me again. Jack, my sweet husband, died suddenly of a heart attack. On a Monday night at 7 P.M.

A wonderful adult life begins when we face the reality of our aloneness squarely.

we were in a meeting with an architect, going over house plans, and by 10 P.M., that very same evening, I was leaving the emergency room as a widow.

I was in shock. Just as I had wanted to do when I was ten years old, I felt like screaming. Why hadn't anyone prepared me for this? I was alone. At ten years old, I could put aside the revelation of being a separate human being. As a young widow, aloneness accompanied me every day and everywhere. Aloneness hit me suddenly again, but this time I had to face it.

A wonderful adult life begins when we face the reality of our aloneness squarely. Then we can put our energy into having a fabulous day, whether we're with someone or not. When we can embrace our singleness, even though we may not always like it, we rise to the grandness that one human being can become.

try this

1. Repeat "Yikes! I'm alone! Yikes! I'm alone!" until it doesn't freak you out to say it.
2. Stand alone for five minutes and look up at the night sky. What do you see? Each star is shining alone and among the others. Even though you may not have realized it completely, you're a bright star too.
3. Learn the formula: One needy person plus one needy person adds up to two needy people. One satisfied person plus one satisfied person adds up to two satisfied people.
4. Proceed in the direction of independence. Whatever you want to do, go for it now.
5. Start a singles discussion group. Make "Yikes! I'm Alone" one of the topics. Ask members to bring poems or thoughts to share about the topic. Serve good treats.

We are unutterably alone, essentially, especially in the things most intimate and most important to us.

—Rainer Maria Rilke

Think of Your Life As a Movie

It was a crystal clear, sunny morning—the kind of morning that persuades you that Puget Sound is heaven. Looking across the lake, I could see the sculpted outline of familiar downtown buildings. In the distance, Mount Rainier stood like a Greek god reigning over his kingdom. The scene was postcard flawless, with periwinkle sky and silky-smooth water—a perfect backdrop for a movie, I thought. Many movies are made in Seattle, but the one that popped immediately to mind was *Sleepless in Seattle* with Tom Hanks and Meg Ryan. I liked that movie. It was predictable, it was romantic, it had a happy ending. Not like my life.

There was nothing predictable about my life these days. My first husband, Jack, the man of my dreams—who, by the way, was movie-star gorgeous—had died suddenly. Full of grief, I married my second husband, Tom, but after two painful years of wedded torture, he ran away with the wife of his best friend, our savings, our boat, and whatever else he could haul away. He left me with bills, a baby, and battered self-esteem. I was not a happy camper. Frankly, I was a basket case. In the space of five minutes I could slide from slight melancholy to catatonic desolation. At the slightest provocation, I could jump from mild annoyance to steely, "Don't mess with me" rage. I wish my life was a romantic comedy, but I'm the antithesis of a blonde, dimple-faced, pencil-thin leading lady. I'm a dark, chubby brunette.

When things are falling apart, however, I'm perfectly capable of putting on a cheerful face. I've been told that I have acting potential. I can look on the bright side, see the silver lining, pull myself up by my bootstraps. My emotions show on my face, but I'm good at faking it, too. It's the leading-lady way that I was conditioned to handle disappointment, but inside, more often than not, I'm anxious and gloomy.

I sometimes visualize my life as scenes from movies. Like the one in *A Star is Born,* when Kris Kristofferson is killed in a car wreck. That scene sends me into wailing fits of air-gasping sobs. In Elisabeth Kübler-Ross's week-long death and dying work-shop, I learned that you can't cry for another person. You can only cry for yourself. It's the spark of sorrow in the other person that ignites the sorrow in you. So when Kris Kristofferson dies unexpectedly in that crash, and when Barbra Streisand has to go on without him, I knew I wasn't distraught over the fate of the actors or the characters they portrayed. No, I was terrified, terri-fied that I had to go on without my sweetheart.

I was grief-stricken and married to a man I didn't respect, couldn't talk to, and had nothing in common with. Even though it was almost midnight when we left the theater, I put on my sunglasses, and Tom and I drove home in silence. I threw myself face down on the bed and curled into a ball. It would make a great movie scene. It was the beginning of the end of our marriage.

No doubt about it, we all have a story to tell that is worthy of the silver screen. That's life—agony and humor juxtaposed with pain. It gives us depth; it gives us perspective; it makes us think of the great heroines and heroes—and the stories they have told us. Some days, thinking of it in that way makes it easier to get out of bed and keep life's disappointments and the daily ups and downs in perspective. Then, no matter what's happening on the periphery, we can stay detached, as if we're sitting surrounded by an audience watching the stories of our lives unfold. When we're in the middle of the heartache, we're like any great actor; we have to go into the pain totally and express it fully. In doing so, we begin the process of healing. It's

> **When we're in the middle of the heartache, we're like any great actor.**

when we don't express our pain that our life becomes a continual drama. It's in the acknowledging of our situation that we're able to rise above it and turn our heartbreak into heartwarming victory. We can be in pain and know that something positive will come out of it. When we view our life as a movie, we can play our role well, but not get stuck in it or typecast. Like those great actors, we trust that sooner or later another good role will come our way.

My client Meghan's story would make a great movie, too. The details of her wedding day are startling, her courage and maturity inspiring. On the morning of their wedding day, Meghan's fiancé announced that he couldn't go through with the marriage. He asked to be let out of it. She couldn't believe what he was saying—it took several hours for the ramifications to sink in. She was angry, she cried, she kicked the air in front of him. Then, amazingly, she took a deep breath, gave him a long reassuring hug and told him that he was free to go. She took a shower, called her parents and bridesmaids, and told them the shocking news. Everyone was dumbfounded. Still, they pulled together and agreed not to let the runaway groom ruin a perfectly lovely party. They didn't have the wedding, but they had the celebration. Meghan attended, held her head up high, and greeted all the guests. They toasted her and danced. They took up a collection and sent her and the maid of honor on a trip to Puerto Vallarta.

Great literature, poetry, and movies are filled with broken hearts and shattered dreams. Beautiful love stories don't necessarily have happy endings. And still the resilience of the human spirit is amazing! When you're having a bad day, step back and observe what's going on around you. Watch what's happening as if it were a scene in a movie. From this perspective, you'll have a more objective view and you're likely to feel less devastated.

I don't know how the story of my life will end, and you don't know how yours will end either. But one thing we can decide together is that we're going to give Academy Award performances in which our spirit triumphs in the end. No long-suffering, mediocre soap-opera parts for us. Let's stay involved in all of life, but not attached to the drama.

try this

1. Write down the names of actors and actresses that you'd choose to play the characters in your life story.
2. Think about the main themes.
3. Carry a journal, and jot down your best lines.
4. For one week, step back and watch. View your life as if you were sitting in the audience.
5. Give yourself a round of applause or, better yet, a standing ovation.

And the story of a love is not important—what is important is that one is capable of love. It is perhaps the only glimpse we are permitted of eternity.

—HELEN HAYES

On My Own

Jogging along the shores of Lake Washington, in my hometown of Kirkland, I felt the familiar lump of despair that had permanently settled in my chest rise to my throat. I was on the verge of screaming, "Hey, what did I do wrong?" As a thirty-five-year-old woman with a one-year-old baby, I often felt as if the best years of my life were over. I ached for the carefree, happily married days of my twenties. I wanted to belong to someone, to be part of a couple. I adored my daughter, but I didn't know if I could manage parenting all alone. I was drowning in bills—leftovers from my second marriage, a rebound that ended in divorce. I had a master's degree, but didn't have a job. My future looked bleak, and I was scared.

Everywhere I looked, there were hand-holding couples or families picnicking with kids. Running past Houghton Beach, I tried not to notice the healthy, pretty young women and handsome, athletic young men playing volleyball. But I always noticed, and just like all the other times that I had before, I felt conspicuous and out of place. I was both a widow and a divorcée. Who would want me? Young families socialize with other young families. Couples invite couples over for dinner. Nonmarrieds with no kids hang out with other nonmarrieds with no kids. "Yes, indeed," I thought, "I don't belong."

I was living week to week, barely getting by. I wished for someone to help me, to chip in with the work and the burden of bills. But there was no one I could turn to, no one to lean on, no one to talk things over with. My neighbors and friends were busy with their own lives; I couldn't expect them to figure out mine.

I pushed myself to run a little faster in hopes that painkilling endorphins would mercifully kick in. My goal was to run from Marina Park to the freeway and back—a total of four miles. I'd only been running for a short time. Just nine months previous, in an attempt to get in shape after an emergency C-section, I'd started my training program. Each evening at around 10 P.M., after Manda was safely sleeping in her crib, I'd step outside and run as far as I could. In the beginning I could only jog from my front door to the cul-de-sac, which was half a block, exactly four house lengths. Then I'd walk the same short distance back home and repeat the routine the next night. I was dedicated, and slowly, my distance increased until here I was, running four miles. "Good for me," I thought. Running helped me stop thinking. It cleared out the anguish of feeling tossed aside. So every other day, whether I could afford it or not, I hired Cecelia to watch Manda for two hours so that I could go for a run.

After my run, I bought half a turkey sandwich and an iced tea from Hoffman's bakery and took it to my favorite picnic-table retreat to write in my journal. My entries typically began with the complaint of the day. "I hate my life." "I hate job hunting." "No one cares about me." "I don't have any money." But this time, for some unconscious reason, I didn't begin that way. Instead I wrote the words "ON MY OWN" in big bold letters across the top of the page.

Seeing those three little words, "on my own," stunned me. I guess I'd never really faced that reality head-on before. Usually I deal with unpleasant situations by pushing them away. I'm better at denial than facing stark reality. Like looking at the sun, I can't view it straight on. I have to look at it from the side or sneak a peek.

Friends and acquaintances enabled me to keep my bias of reality askew, too. If I complained that I was having a rough week, or that I hated being single, they'd say something like, "You're young, you won't be alone for long." Such soothing affirmations kept me holding on to the illusion that this was not my life, that I really didn't have to face being on my own. All that I needed to do was to get by, get by until someone showed up, someone who would pitch in and take care of me.

This journal entry was different. Perhaps the physical challenge of running gave me a boost of emotional courage because this time I didn't shrink away from the truth. I looked at the words squarely, took them in, and let them roll around until they found a corner of acceptance. "Yes, I am on my own," I whispered to myself. "In fact, I've been on my own for six years." I thought. Oh sure, I'd had a brief second marriage, but he was better at avoiding than I was— he was an expert. Whenever there was something he didn't want to face, he'd chug down double bourbon-and-cokes until amnesia set in. I couldn't count on him for much. The day Manda was born, I couldn't reach him by telephone, so I drove myself thirty minutes across the Evergreen Floating Bridge to Virginia Mason Hospital. When I got there, Dr. Carlson, said, "My goodness, you're dilated to eight."

"Yes, I am on my own," I whispered to myself.

"Surely, Judy," I thought, "if you can drive a car while in labor, you can conquer daily living." With that declaration I felt exhilarated, as if I'd been liberated from the clutches of self-doubt. "Never mind that you don't like being on your own," I wrote. "The point is that you are." "Accept it," I said out loud. And with that command, underneath the bold "ON MY OWN" heading, I began to list the feats that I'd accomplished just that week.

1. I'd called the IRS and spoken to an auditor. I'd been avoiding this call for months. (I won't go into all the boring details here. I'll just say that they'd put a lien on the house because my ex hadn't filed the taxes.) I pleaded my case carefully, and two days later they agreed to pursue my ex instead of me.
2. I'd read the instructions and put a baby swing together.
3. I'd mailed my resume.
4. I thought about getting a roommate.

From that day on, whenever I faced a dreaded chore or completed a task that I'd been putting off, I'd list it in my journal. Sometimes when I was feeling overwhelmed, I'd read the list. Over the next several years, the list grew, and each tiny accomplishment empowered me—I was going to make it after all.

try this

1. List five things that you've accomplished on your own. It doesn't matter how small or insignificant they are, just write them down.

2. Buy a package of gold stars, and paste one by each item on your list.
3. Write down one thing that you are thinking about tackling.
4. Make an *On My Own* collage. Cut out pictures and words from magazines that represent what you want for your life. Paste them on a poster board and hang it where you can see it every day.
5. Say to yourself, even if you don't believe it: "I am going . . . to make it!"

> If you haven't had at least a slight poetic crack in the heart, you have been cheated by nature.
>
> —PHYLLIS BATTELLE

Be a One-Carat Person

My decision to become a one-carat woman didn't occur to me until I tried to hock the diamond engagement ring that my second husband had given me. I needed money badly. My part-time job as a social worker in a youth diversion program didn't cover my expenses. Since I wasn't ready to look for another job or to leave my baby with a full-time sitter, I decided to let the ring go. Diamonds are a good investment, and mine was a clear white one-carat. I was confident that I'd get enough cash to get me through another six months, maybe even a year. It was my first and only diamond ring. My first husband and I had worn matching gold bands. At age twenty-three, it was all we could afford. We were frugal, and during the six years of our marriage we preferred to put our money elsewhere. We bought a house, a sailboat, and invested in stocks. Jack surprised me on our fifth anniversary with tiny diamond stud earrings. Those earrings spoke volumes. Jack was so proud that he'd saved his weekly pocket money to buy them. They were the symbol that our love was strong.

Still, secretly I must have wanted a big engagement ring. A big diamond was like a seal of approval announcing to the world that I was desirable. So when Tom began pressuring me to get married, I remember saying, "I'll answer that question when I have a solitaire on my finger." I said it often enough that he must have decided it was the only way to break down my resistance. I was full of grief when I accepted it. I was unsure of what my feelings really were for Tom, but I was alone and grieving. When he took that ring out of its black velvet box, my good judgment melted. The ring sparkled, and I acquiesced. I knew it wasn't wise to marry on the rebound. But in spite of my reservations about our differences, I accepted the ring and secretly hoped that Tom would change his irresponsible ways. I hoped that my determination would be enough to make our marriage successful.

> When he took that ring out of its black velvet box, my good judgment melted.

Since it's much easier to get into a marriage than it is to get out, it took a couple of years for us to go our separate ways. Throughout the separation and divorce, I kept the ring safely hidden in my drawer until I needed money. I wasn't exactly eager to let the ring go, but on the other hand I wasn't attached to it, either. After all, I'd stopped wearing it long before the divorce papers were filed. The only value the ring had for me was as a contribution toward my daughter's education. I needed money.

My ex wasn't paying child support, and my credit cards were maxed. My parents would probably have come to my rescue if they had known how shaky my finances were, but I thought that since I had gotten myself into this mess, I should get myself out.

It was a gray, rainy day when I finally found my courage. I took the ring from its hiding place in a roll of toilet paper underneath the sink, put Manda in her stroller, and made our first and last visit to a store called A Yuppie Pawnshop. The ad in the Yellow Pages proclaimed that all quality items would be considered. It would be easy. There was no qualifying, just instant cash. I was embarrassed that I'd married Tom in the first place, and walking into a pawnshop to sell my engagement ring was like rubbing salt into an open wound.

From the parking lot, I could see through the windows that the store was empty. What a relief, I thought. No waiting, no inquisitive looks from other customers. I'd sneak in and out quickly. I was beginning to feel better. "Manda," I said. "Do you want to go to the children's hour at the library when we're done?"

"Can I help you?" the man from behind the counter asked cheerfully. He didn't fit my image of a pawnshop owner. He looked Ivy League, dressed in his pressed khakis, navy sweater, and polished loafers. In other circumstances I would have made conversation, asked him why he got into the business, and chatted for a while. But on this occasion I was withdrawn and shut down. I could barely muster a smile. "I'd like to sell my ring," I said. "Let's take a look." In the back room I watched as he pulled out his loupe and examined all sides. It didn't take long. "Did you know this is a cubic zirconium?" He must have been able to tell by my blank stare because he didn't wait for an answer. "The band's fourteen karat. I can give you thirty-five bucks." I said nothing. I was humiliated. The sham of my second marriage was out in the open. I was glad that Manda was too young to understand that her father had con-man tendencies and that her mother had been so afraid to be on her own that she'd married him, spent years covering up, pretending to be happy, trying to make him look good, putting on a happy front. No doubt about it—I was a codependent. I had a lot of work to do on myself.

"Thank you for your time." I said. "I'll keep the ring." And I did keep the ring. I have it to this day. It's stored in a safety deposit box. I don't want to risk losing it or having it stolen. It's precious to me. It motivated me to become authentic.

try this

1. Think about this: Is there anything about your life that you've been trying to hide? Perhaps this is the time to face it.
2. Take one courageous step to bring it out of hiding.
3. Call a friend who believes in you and confess your secret.
4. Remember that millions of people are in relationships because they are afraid to be alone. Do you know anyone who suffers from this?
5. Know that your value is not measured by the ring on your finger or the things that you own.

Life is not the way it's supposed to be. It's the way it is.
The way you cope with it is what makes the difference.

—VIRGINIA SATIR

Don't Be Defined by Your Marital Status

Margaret was always "seeing" someone and right after she got engaged to Earl, she seemed even more obsessed with my marital status than she was when we were both unattached. "Do you really want to stay single the rest of your life?" she'd ask, not waiting for the answer. Her questions were endless: "Have you ever thought of joining a singles' club?" "Who's your type, Judy?" "Have you tried speed dating?" "Judy, do you have a date tonight?" If I answered no, she twisted the knife a little deeper. "I don't have the temperament to stay home on Friday night like you do."

This line of questioning is all too prevalent, and it starts all too young. When my daughter, Amanda, was around ten years old, people would actually ask her if she had a boyfriend yet. Even family members at family gatherings teased her, asking "Manda, who's your boyfriend?" By the age of twelve, Amanda knew that the first question her aunts would ask was, "Do you have a boyfriend?" Amanda learned to brace herself for that question, but she never liked it. "Why does it matter?" Amanda asked me. "Why don't they ask me about the fact that I was elected student-body vice president?" Or, "Why don't they ask me about moving my bedroom to the basement?"

Amanda's question, "Why does she always ask if I have a boyfriend?" is a good question. Why are people so concerned with a single person's relationship status? Even Oprah has to deal with the question. On a Larry King interview, she said that people are more concerned about whether she and Stedman are going to get married than if she and Stedman are happy together.

Putting on my psychotherapist hat for a moment, it seems to me that the question reveals something about the person asking it. For example, the people asking such a question may be preoccupied with their own lack of contact with the opposite sex, or maybe they've been reading too many romance novels. Maybe they have a sadistic side and take pleasure seeing someone squirm. Dave, a friend of mine, always asks about my love life. He says that's because "It's more interesting than hearing about my work." Anthropologists might say the question is in the genes; after all, we're biologically programmed to reproduce. Whatever the reasons, the question is here to stay. As a single, I've dealt with it by developing my "Who do you have in mind?" response.

I'm frequently hired as an inspirational speaker, so I know the importance of timing. In my presentations I give pointers on how we can all overcome heartache and disappointment. I offer encouragement that regardless of our circumstance, we can all live a creative life full of joy and service. I use personal stories to illustrate my themes. I tell how my first husband died, how my second ran away with my first husband's money, and how I struggle as a single mother to raise a child and build a satisfying career. At the end, I answer questions from the audience, and someone always asks me about my marital status. "Have you remarried?" they want to know. I don't mind the question at all anymore because I have honed my answer carefully. I pause long enough to make sure that I have everyone's focused attention. Then I smile, and looking directly at the person who asked the question, I say, "Who do you have in mind?" It works every time. The audience bursts into laughter and applause and I'm able to move on to the next question in good spirits. I use that answer whenever I'm asked about my status. It keeps the possibilities open. On more than one occasion, that little sentence, "Who did you have in mind?" planted a matchmaking seed in the person asking it, and later they introduced me to a man whom I was very happy to get to know. "Who did you have in mind?" works with Margaret too. It stumps her every time.

try this

1. Memorize a comeback for the question, "Are you dating anyone?"

2. Practice saying it out loud in front of a mirror. Remember that timing and presentation are important when delivering the line. Practice until your response is upbeat so that you don't come across as defensive.

3. Remember, just because someone asks you a question, that doesn't mean you have to answer. You can get out of answering by turning the tables and asking, "Why do you ask?"

4. Make it a policy to never ask single people (unless, of course, you are the best of friends) if they are dating. If they want you to know, they will volunteer the information.

5. Measure your success on what you're doing, not who you're dating.

If a person loves only one other person and is indifferent to all others, his love is not love, but a symbiotic attachment or an enlarged egotism.

—ERICH FROMM

Woe Is Me

Alice was fifty-seven years old when she came to counseling. Her lawyer recommended that she pull herself together before going before the judge for the property settlement phase of her divorce. Her classic navy-blue suit, high heels, and matching leather handbag gave a first impression that she had it all together.

Alice's husband of thirty-six years moved in with a younger woman just before Valentine's Day. He returned home for the month of March and again for their anniversary, the first week of June. She'd threatened him with financial ruin and made a meek attempt to cut her wrists. She confronted his girlfriend and called her "The Slut." When she talked about her husband, she twisted her diamond wedding band around and around until her finger was raw and red. She swallowed and pulled at her throat instead of crying. She wouldn't allow herself to cry. Eventually she agreed to the divorce and got a big settlement.

Following the divorce, Alice came to counseling every week for two and a half years, and we got to know each other well. Her theme was always the same. "I'll never find another man." She was certain that she'd be more attractive if she had a face-lift, then it was a tummy tuck, then a series of liposuctions. She retold the details of their marriage, about his drinking and his nasty ways of belittling her. She wasn't happy when she had him, but she was even more miserable without him. "I'm the kind of woman who needs a man," she said. She wouldn't or couldn't see any other avenue for happiness. While I understood that "got-to-have-a-man" anguish, I couldn't eliminate hers.

The lack of a man to love was torment. It was painful. It was hot, she could feel it under her skin. Her stomach was upset, and she couldn't sleep through the night. Her two grandchildren brought her no comfort. "I'm not the grandma type," she said.

"I'll never be with another man"; "I'm too old"; "Men don't like me," and various other forms of "It's too late for me" were the topic of each session. "I'm almost sixty. Men aren't interested in old ladies." She was in deep despair, convinced she was no longer capable of being desirable.

For Alice, Saturday night was the hardest. Even though she had standing invitations for dinner with her friends or her children, she'd refuse. In her slump of depression, she stayed in her robe all day and slept on the couch until Sunday morning. Then she'd get dressed and go to church. "I'll never have fun again," she said. "That's a painful thought," I said. She nodded in agreement. "Do you feel it's too late?" I asked. Again she nodded, yes. "Aren't there any exceptions?" I asked. "Maybe for movie stars," she answered. "Really, Judy, do you know a man who'd be interested in me?"

It was a tough question. Many of my clients believe it's getting too late for them too. Earlier that day I'd met with a twenty-seven-year-old woman whose four-year relationship just ended. As she cried, she voiced the same "I'm too old" apprehension. When she dried her tears, I said, "You're sad and scared; you're in transition."

It wasn't just women who were lonely. Clark was thirty-seven when he came for counseling. A single father, raising two young children, he didn't have time or money for a social life. Clark's mother took care of the kids during the week. On the weekends, Clark had them by himself. "Women aren't interested in a geek with no money and two kids," he'd say.

My clients had much in common—conditioning that tied their happiness to a man or a woman, the fear of being alone, the anguish of loss, and not knowing where to turn for comfort. But they were different, too. Their pain was as personal as finding their way through it would be.

Alice cried and cried. She'd get angry, and sometimes we'd disagree. "Alice," I'd say, "are you as frustrated with this broken record as I am?" "Alice, can't you see any other possibilities for happiness?" "Alice, if you're convinced that you'll never have another man, don't you want to make sure that what life you do have is satisfying?"

Wasting energy wishing for something you don't have while ignoring all that you do have is a vicious mental trap. Grieving for what you've lost and for what you imagined that you might never have again is a step toward liberation. For Alice and Clark, focusing on the possibility that they may never have another relationship was essential. Countless times Alice said, "I'll never have another man." And countless times I answered, "You may be right," or "I can't predict the future, but it's true, you are alone right now."

> **Wasting energy wishing for something you don't have while ignoring all that you do have is a vicious mental trap.**

It was in those moments of the truth that we connected. She'd look at me, I'd look at her, and there was nothing left to say. She settled down, and we'd sit together in silence. It was the same with Clark. He hadn't chosen singleness either. He'd wanted to be dad, but not a single parent. "It isn't fair," he'd say, and then he'd try to convince me that he couldn't do it all alone. "You are doing it," I'd say. "Yup," he'd say, "but I don't have to like it."

And so it is with many singles. You don't want to be alone. You didn't choose it, and you don't like it. It's natural to grieve and grumble about it. It's paradoxical and a bit like magic, because it's through acknowledging the stark reality of aloneness that life becomes bearable.

Eventually Alice got her energy back, joined a singles group, and saw a psychic. The psychic said she'd travel and meet plenty of people. Alice took up bridge again. She bought a mobile home in a retirement community and moved to Arizona. The last time I saw Alice she'd softened. "I live alone," she said. Then she winked at me and added, "But I'm too busy to be lonely."

try this

1. Give yourself permission to talk about your fears of being alone. Everyone goes through times when they feel hopeless.
2. Know that coming to terms with the reality of your situation is a task of growing up; doing so allows you to move forward.
3. Read the book *Man's Search for Meaning,* by Victor Frankel. It helped me come to terms with suffering.
4. Consider seeing a therapist, a psychic, and a tarot card reader. Hearing from another person that there is hope for you might be the optimistic boost you need.
5. Get a massage. You'll feel better when your body feels better. When you're grieving any loss, touch is very important for healing.

A broken heart is what makes life so wonderful five years later, when you see the guy in an elevator and he is fat and smoking a cigar and saying 'Long time no see.'

—PHYLLIS BATTELLE

The Key to Single Contentment

It's hard to surrender to singleness when we've all been shoved and pushed into coupling. We cling to what's familiar. We long for happiness, but we tell ourselves that we can't be happy unless we have a lover or a spouse. It takes determination to rid ourselves of all our preconceived notions, resistances, and myths about being single. But we have to do it because that's the key to contentment.

Twenty-three-year-old Michelle came for counseling after her breakup with her first love. Crying, she said, "I don't want to end up an old maid." "Where did you get that notion?" I asked. For a brief moment she looked stunned at my question, but she shrugged it off. A month later, she'd met another guy and no longer had the desire for counseling. A year later, however, she was back voicing the same old-maid anguish. That's how silent myths work. They pop up and feed our despair, and unless we bring them out and replace them with something more affirming, they keep tumbling through our consciousness, inflicting unnecessary torment.

The shopworn images of an old maid with a houseful of cats and of a dirty, cantankerous old man are myths of long ago. The one-dimensional view of the swinging single is a distortion as well. Singleness encompasses so much more than these narrow perspectives suggest. If we buy into them, we allow these myths to keep us frozen like little ice statues, unable to embrace all the people and joy around us.

There are a myriad of beliefs to free ourselves from, such as these old saws: "You're selfish if you're single"; "If you're not married by such and such age, you're over the hill"; "If you're young and single, you're hip"; "If you're old and single, you're lonely"; "If you're single, you're undesirable"; "If you're single, you're defective or incomplete"; or "If you're single it's because you can't settle down." We have to clear ourselves of all of these notions because they have nothing to do with who we are.

Twenty-seven-year-old Eleanor isn't sure she ever wants to be married. She says, "I don't need to be married to feel complete. I think feeling whole depends on me." Eleanor says that people don't always believe her when she tells them that she isn't drawn toward marriage. There are

The single stigma is outdated.

cynics everywhere who are convinced that life is incomplete unless you're married with kids. They want everyone to settle down. Eleanor isn't persuaded, though. She knows what's right and true for her. She's independent and doesn't have to conform to feel satisfied.

There are more singles now than ever. Fifty percent of your married friends will become single through divorce. Of those who remain together, fifty percent will become suddenly single by being widowed.

Singles are everywhere, doing all the things that people do. The single stigma is outdated. People no longer look down on singles as they once did. Singles are vital and involved in all segments of society. Being single is not bad; it's not awful. It does not mean that you're unlovable, undesirable, or antisocial. It does not mean that something is wrong with you. It doesn't mean that you'll end up friendless and abandoned. Single is your fundamental condition, and chances are that you'll be single more than once in your life. So throw away your negative beliefs, and replace them with a philosophy that enhances your well-being.

Consider this. There are happy singles and unhappy singles; there are happy marrieds and unhappy marrieds; there are happy living-aloners and unhappy living-aloners. Regardless of your single status, choose happy.

try this

1. Take a long sheet of butcher paper, a big black marking pen, and chart your single history.

My single history goes like this: Born single, married, single the second time through death of my husband, married the second time, single the third time following divorce. Single and taking a sabbatical from dating, then single and dating for four years. Single and living together for ten years and single again following my partner's death. Now I'm single, living alone, and thrilled.

2. Be on the lookout for limiting myths about singleness, and don't go there! List any myths that bug or haunt you. Replace any negative ideas about a bleak future with one that's rosy.
3. Write this sentence 100 times: "I'm proud to be Satisfied, Fulfilled, and Independent."

4. Spread uplifting stories about singleness.
5. Read the poet Rainer Maria Rilke for inspiration.

> During your best years you don't need a husband.
> You do need a man, of course, every step of the way,
> and they are often cheaper emotionally and a lot more
> fun by the dozen.
>
> —HELEN GURLEY BROWN

It's Hard to Be Single, Sometimes

Let's not sugarcoat it. It's hard to be single sometimes. It truly is. It's especially hard when the appliances aren't working. When the seal on the upstairs toilet cracked and water leaked down the wall onto Marie's velvet coat hanging in the closet on the floor below, she was definitely distraught that there was no man around to show her how to turn off the water. On the positive side, she did figure out that the main valve is located in the laundry room, which it turns out she needed to know when the water heater burst a few months later.

The mouse was a completely different story. Marie couldn't think of one advantage to being single when a mouse ran through her kitchen. She really couldn't handle that. She freaked out and ran next door. John came over, stuck cheese in a trap, and told her to call him when the mouse died. "How will I know, if there's a dead mouse in the trap?" Marie asked, suspecting all along that she already knew the answer. "You'll have to look," he said in a way that suggested she was making too much fuss.

Marrieds have no idea of the challenges that singles face. Singles become geniuses at daily living. They have to. Couples are quite spoiled. Singles either learn how to do things they don't want to do, beg a friend to help, or hire someone. At the very least, when you're part of a couple, there's always someone to complain to—if you've chosen well, they'll even come to your rescue. Singles can't pass the chore off or plead helplessness. No, they have to mop up their own messes.

> **Singles become geniuses at daily living. They have to.**

It's not that singles object to learning new skills, it's just that unexpected breakdowns can throw us for a loop. One cold winter morning when Sydney's car wouldn't start, she naturally reached for her cell phone to call Dad. It was her automatic, unconscious response. But as she pulled it from her purse, she reminded herself, "Whoops, I don't live in the same town as Dad anymore." After graduate school, Sydney had moved away from her hometown, and this was her first car crisis. "I had a good cry," she said, "because Dad couldn't come to my rescue."

That's the kind of malfunction that really rattles us, those unforeseen breaks in our infrastructure. All those things our parents did that made life easier, the things we took for granted when we were living under their roof, now clearly are our responsibilities. Mark graduated with high marks from law school, but when he wanted to eat something other than a frozen dinner, he was stumped. He'd known that his mom was a good cook, but until he tackled cooking for himself, he hadn't appreciated what went on behind the scenes to put a meal together.

There are so many tasks of daily living to master—from hanging pictures alone, to grocery shopping for one. Top that off with unexpected annoyances, and it's enough to make you wonder why you moved away from home in the first place. Our parents don't want us to have any kind of discomfort, so they pray that we settle down so our spouse can take up where they left off. The jobs that the opposite sex used to handle are the ones that seem most daunting. If Dad took care of the car and now you have to do it, it requires almost overwhelming effort on your part to figure out what needs to be done.

There's nothing wrong with commiserating about tiny irritants or big annoyances. In fact, we bounce back quicker voicing our laments than leaving them to fester under the surface. My friend Dan called me just the other morning and said, "I forgot to buy coffee beans." Then he added, "If I had a wife that wouldn't happen. She'd say, 'Dan, don't forget to buy coffee beans,' and it would all be taken care of." Then he paused and added gleefully, "Or she'd be nagging me to give up caffeine."

try this

1. Admit when you're having a difficult day. If someone asks how you're doing, say, "I'm having a difficult day."
2. Commiserate wisely. Telling a couple isn't always the best choice, as single amnesia has probably set in. It's best to talk to someone who has been through what you're going through. Who is that for you?

3. Ask for assistance with tasks of daily living such as turning the mattress, cleaning out the gutters, or hanging a mirror. Neighbors and friends are willing to pitch in when they know what you need. It's also a good idea to get a good fix-it book.

4. Set a good mood for your home and your car by playing upbeat background music.

5. Buy yourself an enormous bouquet of flowers, and put one bud in a little plastic vase on the dashboard of your car.

> Everything that happens to you is your teacher. The secret is to learn to sit at the feet of your own life and be taught by it.
>
> —POLLY BERRIEN BERENDS

Lessons and Bright Spots

Often, when I ask people to tell me about being single, they tell me about their relationships. That's because single and relationships go together. Listen carefully, and you'll notice that when people talk about being single, they mention a former boyfriend or girlfriend. They talk about the one that ended or the one they want someday. Likewise, when you think about relationships, a curtain of singleness hangs in the background. Couples sometimes stay in relationships because they're afraid of being alone, and others stay single for fear of losing themselves in a bad marriage.

Being single is natural, as natural as being together, and you'll probably have a go-around at both. One is not better, and one is not worse. Instead, they're complementary. There are bright spots and lessons in both. Just be where you are. It's when we resist the lessons and benefits that we suffer. The mind can be tricky. It craves what it imagines is missing. Singles crave commitment; marrieds think about freedom.

At age twenty-four, Annie had an epiphany and told me about it. "I've realized," she said, "that my life can be exciting without a meaningful relationship. This is a liberating perspective for me, because I've lived under the old way of thinking for so long. I don't really know how to go about life without wondering if I'll meet my match soon. I've always been planning for the eventual meeting of one right person, as if marriage should be entering the picture at some point. Now that I can see another possibility, it seems like my real life is beginning."

> Being single is natural, as natural as being together, and you'll probably have a go-around at both.

Making the choice to be single is often the best choice. "Until the right person comes along, I'm enjoying the benefits of being single," Eric told me. "I went through a divorce when I was twenty-eight and now I think a twenty-year-old is better off staying single. I was in a hurry and it only brought me pain in the end. There are many fun things to do, and people to do those things with without having to be married. I'll know when that right person comes along. It may not be for another ten years. Until then, I'm enjoying my time. Once I'm married, I'll probably miss my own time."

All of us know what a delicious temptation it can be to beat ourselves up about almost anything that goes wrong. Your relationship ends, and you didn't try hard enough or you tried too hard and stayed in it too long. Forty-four-year-old Tina told me, "It took me seventeen years of a bad marriage to figure out that I could have a wonderful life being single. I've been dating again and have met two wonderful guys who are very opposite. What a blast I'm having with no strings. If marriage happens, that would be somewhere down the road, but for now single life is just too good to mess it up."

It's out of troubling times that we learn the most about ourselves. That's when the bright spots show up. Forty-seven-year-old Stephanie is doing that for the first time. "When I got married at nineteen, I put my energy into raising a family and now that they're independent, I'm moving to France. I've studied French for eight years, I've put my all belongings in storage, and rented a furnished flat in the heart of Paris. Now that I'm single I have a chance to explore another side of myself. I feel a little guilty, but I'm doing it."

The journey of your own becoming begins with recognition: "This *is* my life." Fifty-five-year-old Irene told me, "Nope!" She isn't going to get married again. When I asked why, she said, "It takes a mighty good man to beat no man at all." When I asked her what she meant, she said she's had men who cheat, men who lie, men who lie around the couch all day, men who took her money, and men who treated her poorly. Now that she's older and again single, she said it would take a mighty good man for her to give up her single life, which is now stable, orderly, under control, and peaceful.

We all have lessons to learn. Sometimes we need to be alone to learn these lessons, and sometimes we need to be part of a couple. So it's important to trust the process and the journey—you never know where it can lead you. If you're alone at this junction, trust that this is where you need to be. Trust that when you are ready for a new love, you will find each other. That's the way the universe works. Learn the lessons of being single, enjoy all the bright spots, and know that good things are coming your way.

All of our experiences shape us. They are molding us into the person we're becoming.

try this

1. Don't take your singleness for granted. It's easy in the press of daily life to overlook how much you are enjoying being on your own.

2. Praise the ordinary lessons you're learning. Is there is one thing that you're learning by being on your own that you couldn't learn being part of a couple?

3. Notice the bright spots in your day. Talk about them and be an encouragement to others.

4. If you want to talk about your former lover, or former husband, it's perfectly okay—as long as your intent is on learning a lesson!

5. Be easy on yourself. Remember, all birth is painful.

There came a time when the risk to remain tight in the bud was more painful than the risk it took to blossom.

—ANAÏS NIN

Dream a New Dream

Mia looked forward to being married. From the time she was a young girl she had been thinking about her wedding day and planning the details carefully. For her sixteenth birthday, her mother—who had encouraged her dream—gave her a hope chest, and for several years they filled it with linens, candlesticks, wineglasses, and beautiful accouterments for her imaginary newlywed home. They both enjoyed the dream.

Mia went to college, and during the final quarter, she fell into a slump. In the recesses of her mind, Mia believed that she couldn't be truly happy until her dream for a husband came true. That summer when she moved into a loft apartment her mother brought the hope chest, brimming full of lovely linens for her. Mia's apartment had a peek-a-boo view of the bay, but she barely noticed because the chest grabbed for her attention. Looking at the hope chest, Mia felt sad about the treasures tucked away and feared that she might never get to enjoy them. Her hope for lasting happiness was tied to her dream of being a couple, and all other dreams were secondary. Would opening the chest now spoil her chances for married bliss later?

She shared her dilemma with friends. Should she keep the household items hidden in her hope chest? Should she send the chest back with her mother, or should she bring the treasures out and use them for herself? She thought about it, wrote about it in her journal, and slowly had a change of heart. "Perhaps," she thought, "true happiness is within my reach." She opened the chest and began using all the beautiful accessories. "I'll pin my hope on me."

We've all done it, pinned our hope for happiness onto someone or something else: "If I had a boyfriend, a girlfriend, the right job, the right car, the right house, and so on, *then* I would be happy." And while it may be true that a nice boyfriend and a shiny car might be great additions, or that a pretty girlfriend and cozy house might bring you satisfaction, what about the in-between times? Are you willing to put happiness on hold for only one dream?

Of course, there's nothing wrong with hoping, visualizing, and dreaming about your future, but please consider for a moment that there are many dreams to dream. The dream that you can only have a real life if you're part of a couple has had a grip on singles of all ages. Fortunately, options are expanding. Life is full of many dreams, and regardless of age or our conditioning, we can pick another one.

How many dreams can you dream? Where are you pinning your hope? What are your aspirations?

try this

1. Ask yourself this question: Do I want to wait for happiness to come along, or do I want to make my own?

2. Start a discussion group and consider this question: Is it possible to be single and have a wonderful life?

3. Buy a wooden box from a craft store, paint it or decorate it, and then label it "My Many, Many Dreams."

4. List your dreams and hopes on tiny slips of paper and put them in the box. As you discover new dreams, add those too.

5. Place the box in a prominent spot; once in a while reread, change, and edit your dreams.

There are many wonderful things that will never be done if you do not do them.

—CHARLES D. GILL

The Art of Being Single

Living single, satisfied, fulfilled, and independent is an art. It's not a birthright, an inheritance, or a windfall. It's not luck. It's something that's developed, studied, worked on, and perfected. It requires inventiveness, imagination, determination, awareness, and skill. Anyone with gumption and desire can do it. Anyone who wants to celebrate and rejoice in all the magnificence that life offers can practice the art. Life is overflowing within us and around us, in the clouds, the trees, and in the stars. A satisfied single, like a poet, a musician, or a dancer, is committed to celebrating all of existence. They see beauty in it all. Such a single stands on her own, apart from the crowd. She dances to the beat of her own drum.

Taking responsibility for one's happiness is a big part of the art. Even though the myths of the spinster and dirty old man no longer hold much weight, when it comes right down to it, it still takes practice and courage to be your own person. It's a huge assignment to celebrate when you're feeling shaky. When your psyche is cracked, when your heart is broken, and when the hopes you've built your dreams upon are lying in shambles, that's when true grit and spirit are born. That's when the fine-tuning and polishing of our character starts.

Seventy-one-year-old Irene, widowed for ten years, likes being single and is carefully perfecting the art. "When you're old and single," she told me, "you're allowed to be eccentric and flamboyant." Her husband, Earl, whom she had adored, was a conservative type and squelched her without intending to. Now she gets to bring out her more interesting side. She misses her sweet husband very much, and she deals with her grief by living well. Her weeks are filled with activities. On Sunday nights she reads her poetry at the Globe Café. On Monday morning she exercises, and in the afternoon she tutors an immigrant in English. Two afternoons each week she works behind the counter at the movie theater. It's the part-time job she always wanted but never had because Earl didn't think it was dignified for his wife to work.

> "When you're old and single, you're allowed to be eccentric and flamboyant."

Her friend Lola prefers a slower lifestyle and says, "All I really need is a cozy irresistible bed. I eat lots of munchies there, so I bought myself a big silver bed tray. My favorite bed munchies are twice-baked potatoes with chopped portobello mushroom, onion, thyme, and gorgonzola cheese."

Some folks are convinced that it's impossible to be single and happy. They think that a good life depends on having a partner, a ring, or marriage certificate. They're indoctrinated in the misconception that any single woman who says that she's happy is either deluded, has resigned herself, has given up, or is not telling the truth. They think that any happily single man is afraid of commitment.

Being single is not about having an armful of admirers or a bed full of lovers, nor is it about being a miserable lonely eccentric with cats for companions. A satisfied man isn't out to prove that he's a man because he drives the fastest car or can get any woman he wants. He values honesty and integrity over conquest. A satisfied woman doesn't live her life based on research, statistics, common practices, or what the neighbors might think. She listens to her own wisdom and has the strength to act on it.

A satisfied single rejoices in it all, including the contradictions and paradoxes with which a wonderful life is brimming. The art of singleness begins with the understanding that life is poetry and song, beauty and suffering. If you can be alone and enjoy your own company, then you can be sad and celebrate that, too. If you can stumble and reach out, then you're becoming an artist, painting on your life canvas. Singleness is about becoming more, more than we thought we were, more than we were told we were. Singleness is the art of reaching into the deepest part of ourselves and finding the capacity to met life's challenges with grace.

try this

1. Sign up here. Singleness is an art to be studied and practiced, and you're more than welcome to join those of us who are pursuing the artistry. Go to *www.judyford.com* and take the pledge.

2. Vow to remain pleasant toward fellow students. Men are not the enemy; women are not the enemy.

3. Resolve to be an eager, open-minded student.
4. Purge yourself of bitterness. Do everything you can to get over past injustices.
5. Eliminate negativity. Write down all your negative thoughts about single life. For every negative belief that you have, there's a corresponding positive. Write them down. Carry them with you. Remind yourself of them every day.

> The miracle is not to fly in the air, or to walk on the water, but to walk on the earth.
>
> —CHINESE PROVERB

Every Season Has Its Own Delights

The intoxicating excitement of a twenty-something bachelor or bachelorette is different from the passion of a seasoned fifty-year-old. In your twenties, everything you do is urgent—it's like a matter of life and death. But later on, when you're not quite so keyed up, singlehood has a different dimension, a different flavor. It's more relaxed. It's sweeter. Every season has its own delights, whether it's the ticking biological clock of the thirty-year-old, the onset of a second adulthood in the forties, or the new zest for adventure of a vibrant sixty-year-old. Knowing this and understanding it is vitally important. If you don't, you'll anticipate at fifty what you did at twenty. The needs of a forty-year-old are different from those of a twenty-year-old. Twenty-somethings may be going out four nights a week looking for excitement, while fifty-somethings are content staying closer to home. Mangoes in December might be nice in the supermarket, but when it comes to singleness, the fresh flavors of each decade are the most delicious.

The Decades of Being Single

In every decade of your adult life, being single will carry different obligations as well as different rewards. Read on through the following sections for guidance and a little illumination concerning what you can expect from the decade you're in and the ones to come.

The Steamy Twenties

Ready or not, this is the transition decade. Christen yourself "bachelor" or "bachelorette." As a graduate of the childhood experience, no longer dependent on parental authority, you're on your own and there's a lot of living to do. Like a racehorse at the starting gate, you're ready to run, and with no one holding you back, the possibilities are endless. Hormones are rushing, energy is high, and you're at full speed. Apply your energy toward becoming a feisty, self-assured, autonomous person.

Challenge

Most people are single at this stage, but some folks are already eager to link up, move in, or walk down the aisle. Waiting for romance versus taking charge and making it happen is a delicate maneuver. If you're feeling the pull to mate, it's a good idea to slow down a bit and ask yourself, "Why rush?" An enormous challenge for all twenty-somethings is handling sexuality in a healthy way. The trick is to find the balance between letting off steam and expressing sexuality in a conscious manner, in a way that doesn't harm you or others.

Stop the Pressure

True, the terror of total independence can be overwhelming, and some people hook up in their twenties just to avoid the great unknown—being alone. There's no need to hurry. The twenties are a time of self-discovery, a chance to explore passions and interests in a way you couldn't when you were living with parents or going to school. It is your chance to get absorbed in what excites you.

What to Try

Meet as many people as you can—go on dates, take classes, join a reading group. Give everyone a chance, but don't freak out if you get rejected. Take it in stride, and move on. Meet as many different people as you can because the more experience you have, the better you'll know yourself. Use all that steam to explore options, meet people, make friends, and try new things. This is the decade of being socially active and well rounded.

Reward

Having both personal power and freedom is a lot of fun. Making your own way in the world and having jingle in your pocket and back-up savings are two big measures of your maturity. Maturity and cash are good things to have before you make a commitment to someone else. A side benefit is that if you do decide to get hitched, the older you are when marry the first time, the better your chances are of staying married.

The Whirling Thirties

With so much societal pressure, the thirty-year-old psyche is under siege. This is the decade of "wanting it all"—commitment, family, career, house, great car, and great body. This is the decade of the ticking biological clock. People are starting to pair up and make babies. The stampede to build a nest and start a family is dizzying. For some, it seems like time is running out. There are so many biological obligations that it's possible for your own needs to get lost in the shuffle. With so many pressures, it's easy to forget about what your personal goals are and lose your focus. While compromise does have its payoff, if you're sacrificing what in your heart you know is true, you'll likely get worn out, resentful, and bitter.

Challenge

It's easy to feel left out during this decade if you're not in a relationship. The challenge is not to be swept away by what's expected. No need for apologies. No need for explanations. If you're not ready for a baby, that's okay. If you're yearning for a baby and there's no partner in sight, there are other parenting options to consider. This is a decade of empowerment. It's about learning that there are things in life we can't control. It's about figuring out what we can control and then making the most of things. Most of all, it's about staying on course and being true to your own dreams. Your greatest challenge is to make decisions based on what is right for you.

Stop the Pressure

Take it easy. Don't push yourself to please others —especially when it comes to your decision about marrying and having a child. Be reflective about these biological urges, and avoid the tendency to fall into the pit of thinking time is running out. There's considerable stress from the outside to do what is expected rather than what's right. On this one, pleasing others is not the way to go.

What to Try

If you're still hearing that clock ticking and you find yourself thinking more about babies, that's the pull of biology. Get a puppy or a kitten, and give "parenting" a try. With the biological clock ticking, the tendency may be to rush to have a child before you've considered the ramifications. Instead of letting instinct rule, wait and consider how your life will change as a single parent. Do you want the financial and emotional commitment? Where would you put your energy if you decided not to become a parent? Be thoughtful, and make decisions based on internal reflection, not on external pressures. Nurture a circle of friends who really care about you. Let them become your extended family.

Reward

Making decisions based on what is in your power while letting go of the rest is oh so relaxing. It's surprising how well things work out when you let go of what you can't control. When you stay true to yourself, it's amazing what delightful opportunities come.

The Fabulous Forties

This is the decade of the second adulthood. "Life begins at forty" is the motto. Once you get past the shock of being forty, you find out how satisfying this decade can be. You've set foot in middle age (more or less), yet you still feel like a youngster. It's a surprise to catch a glimpse of yourself in a full-length mirror. You're either terrified of tiny wrinkles and running to a plastic surgeon, or you're thrilled when you're complimented about how young you look. Either way it's time for the three R's: review, revise, and revitalize. Whether you're an original single, divorced, or widowed, here's an opportunity to take dreams off the back burner. With the experience you've got, you can try a new career, date younger, or make peace with your ex.

Challenge

Your goal at this stage is to make conscious choices, rather than slipping into self-defeating behavior. Look around, and you may see relationships growing stale and falling apart. The youthful illusions of a happy forever are crumbling. The challenge is not to get discouraged or overwhelmed by the realization that much of life is accidental, but to be encouraged because there is much that's chosen. You've lived long enough to know that life is both chance and choice. This is the decade of asking, "What it's all about?" and taking charge of what you can control, not fretting over the rest.

Stop the Pressure

Don't compare yourself to younger folks—stop competing. You know yourself, and that's an asset. Instead of pretending, be who you really are. Achievement is great, but inner harmony is grand.

What to Try

Put energy into making and maintaining a variety of friends. Never underestimate the value of good platonic companionship or the energy of hanging around with a good buddy. Apply the three R's: review, revise, revitalize. Review the last three decades. Revise your life plan to fit your new understanding. Revitalize your body, mind, and soul. There's only one way to live well, and that's to be open. Don't get set in your ways. Keep learning, shedding what doesn't fit and fine-tuning yourself.

Reward

As a forty-something, you're more comfortable in your own skin. The old adage—life begins at forty—is true.

Liberating Fifties

This is the "prime-time" decade, so make the most of it. It's great to arrive at fifty, the decade of moving from worry about what others expect to the feeling "This is my time." Fifty-something singles have experience with relationships, children, good times and bad. All that wisdom can be a real enhancement to the pleasures of this decade. Because of the shift away from personal problems to an interest in social change and community involvement, activism is big in this decade. With the mastery you've gained, there's more living to do. Yes, you've done a lot, but you're not done yet.

Challenge

Sexism and ageism may leave a fifty-something feeling vulnerable and invisible. Allow yourself to grieve about it, then allow yourself to move on from it. The upside is that you no longer need to worry about what the crowd thinks. You can think and be your own unique character and that's oh so liberating. The only person to compete with is you. You can find what absorbs you, be unconventional, and indulge your passions. Friendship with both sexes is essential for fulfillment in the fifties.

Stop the Pressure

You've lived a half a century, and you've earned the right to be a character. Hold your head up because there's more living to do. Instead of ruminating about past mistakes, you can make amends and start again. Life gives us many chances to follow our dreams, to reconnect with old friends, to heal our past relationships, and to try moving in a new direction and starting fresh.

What to Try

There's nothing like a liberated, passionate fifty-something. The body has changed, but passion hasn't. Statistics about the lack of potential lovers may discourage you, but there is always an exception and it can be you. Use your wit, charisma, and zest, and you won't be lonely. Pursue your interests, as these are the threads that weave a vibrant community. If it's a lover you're seeking, be lively and playful about it. Write a personal ad and be intriguingly honest. Warmth, aplomb, and curiosity are very appealing.

Reward

With your emotional maturity you have plenty to offer, and the younger generation desperately needs role models who are living fully. Family commitments are first, but after that there's plenty of energy for other pursuits. According to my inside sources, women of this age are quite appealing to younger men. You'll have to do your own research to verify.

Incredible Sixties

Have you noticed how many more singles there are in this decade? Sixty isn't what it used to be. By this decade you know that death is coming, and with that increased awareness there's more emphasis on staying healthy, fit, and vital. Sixty-year-olds are on the go and moving—at the gym, on bikes, walking, hiking, and dancing. Being the breadwinner is no longer the main focus; the emphasis shifts to the needs of body and soul. Sixty-somethings are simplifying and focusing on the core values—creativity, companionship, and celestial matters.

Challenge

While the rewards of being a grandparent are many, the challenge is not to accept a one-dimensional view of yourself. Being of a "certain age" doesn't mean you have to let go of your sensuous side, so hold on to that sparkle! There's more to being sixty than wrinkles and gray hair. Spirituality and meaning are themes. Gratitude is more than lip service. The biggest fear for sixty-year-olds is the fear of becoming isolated from friends or community. Financial pressures often add to the fear of becoming homeless, with not enough resources. More and more sixty-year-olds are remaining in the work force and becoming mentors for the youngsters.

Stop the Pressure

Who cares what people think? That includes your adult children. If you think they'll freak out about what you're up to, don't tell them.

What to Try

Make friends with all ages. Stay active. Resurrect the things of your youth that you didn't get to pursue then, and do them now. Suddenly doing something slightly rebellious, like buying a scooter and riding it, is cool! Whether it's dressing in purple, wearing red shoes, or learning to dance, you can be an interesting character and no one minds. In fact, the more free you are, the more alive you feel. The young folks like it. It gives them hope. If you're looking for romance, try looking up an old flame. Lots of people this age have another go-around at love.

Reward

You're old enough for senior discounts, and that makes a date less expensive. But you might have to ask directly for the discount because sixty-somethings don't look like they used to. By the way, research shows that some men and women in their sixties and beyond are still falling head-over-heels in love and having sexual encounters. Others, however, are so absorbed in their creativity that it would take a highly evolved person to get their attention.

Spontaneous Seventies

This is the season of mellowing. Your attitude and demeanor have softened. Most things aren't worth making a ruckus over. Now instead of fighting and getting all riled up, you're interested in what brings people together. Forgiveness is so sweet. There are many advantages to be seventy and single. You're allowed to be eccentric, to put out your more interesting side and be flamboyant. You're out of the box.

Challenge

You probably never thought you'd be this age and now the challenge is to not isolate yourself. Sure there are younger people everywhere and sometimes you feel invisible, but that can have benefits. You can get away with a lot more. Besides, young people always notice someone with savoir-faire and out of earshot they say things like, "Isn't he in good shape," or "She's sure on the go." The challenge is to approach living with a light heart because by this age you know that it can't be taken seriously. The ability to laugh and see the funny side will take you far.

Stop the Pressure

There are no more deadlines. You don't have to do anything. You can dawdle away the afternoon or putter in your workshop. You can sit and stare for as long as you like. You can think great thoughts, reminisce, do crossword puzzles, or indulge in fanciful dreams.

What to Try

You don't have to answer to anyone, but making amends and building bridges can go a long way toward making this decade peaceful. Don't let grudges stand between you and someone you care about. Accept responsibility for misunderstandings, and apologize for mistakes. There are more singles due to death, and you'll probably lose some of your friends. So reach out in compassion to all those who are having another go-around at being single.

Reward

You may grapple with issues of aging, but there's still a twinkle in your eye. By this time, you know that life is fleeting, and with that understanding you don't want to miss a moment.

Eighty and Beyond

There's only one thing to say, and that is that you've got stories to tell. You're an elder. Now is the time to tell the tales of your history. You've seen a lot, learned a lot, and hopefully you're wiser. Pass on the stories by recording them on audio or writing them down. What a blessed gift!

2

There Are *Places* We All *Have* to Go *Alone*

We are born alone and die alone. In between we have all kinds of relationships, but still there are places in life to which we must go absolutely alone. Your friend can drive you to the dentist, sit in the waiting room, even buy you a milkshake afterward, but you have to sit in the chair all alone.

The good news is that you don't have to have a partner to go the movies, and you don't need a partner to be surrounded in love. Stake your claim on fulfillment, and overcome your fear of singleness. Rather than being weighed down by what you don't have, soar with your talents in tow. Then, regardless of your marital status, you can go anywhere and do anything.

The Most Difficult Decisions Often Turn Out to Be the Most Brilliant

Do you feel a little shaky and unsure of yourself around the opposite sex? Are you confused about the dating scene? After an evening out, do you sometimes feel blah? Are you bored? Have you been dating here and there, but nothing's clicking? Are you caught in the cycle of one bad relationship after another? Are you sick of the bar scene? Tired of meeting through the personals? Have you been taking care of others for so long that you've forgotten what excites you?

That's what's going on with Isabel, and that's why she's taking a sabbatical from dating. Even though she's just coming out of a divorce, she's wishing for a man to rescue her and dreading the possibility at same time. She's ambivalent. She wants a man, but she doesn't. She knows that she's vulnerable; if a man should come along and whisper sweet nothings in her ear, she might follow him anywhere. She needs a shift in perspective, but she can't figure it out while she's dating. The idea of not dating scares her, but it's as if she's standing on the edge of a cliff with a tiger chasing her. Instinctively she makes a decision and jumps to the other side. And so without thinking much about it, she takes a furlough from dating.

Her friend Blaine is vulnerable too. Like Isabel, she's a bundle of needs. It's like that after breakups, and hers was torturous on all fronts. Her husband ran off with another woman, she's moved from a large house to a small condo, put her kids in day care and taken a job. Blaine is tired, overworked, and scared, and so to make herself feel better, she's dating. When her two kids are at their dad's, she goes dancing.

It's not hard for Blaine to meet men, and she has a string of them—Larry, Bill, Joe, and Ed. They look alike and talk alike; they have the same flat personality, just like her ex. Isabel is beginning to see a pattern in her friend's behavior. (It's easier to see other people's patterns than to see our own, isn't it?) "I'm over my ex," Blaine says, when Isabel asks her about it.

Call it women's intuition, divine guidance, common sense, fear, or wising up, but something within Isabel knows that she shouldn't date. She wants to someday, but her marriage taught her that hitching her future on a guy doesn't guarantee a happy ending. Like a pioneer woman crossing the prairie, she needs to blaze her own trail. If she intends to support herself and her daughter in a style that she hopes to become accustomed to someday, she has to develop her potential.

Isabel doesn't have a personal coach, a guide, or a consultant, but she does have a wee small voice inside offering wise counsel. Lots of dates may make you feel needed, and having lots of dates also makes you feel good. But all those dates don't necessarily make you feel good about yourself. And feeling good about yourself is worth far more than just feeling good. If you feel good about yourself, you feel good even when you feel awful. Once you feel good about yourself, even the most horrendous tragedies will not destroy you. When you feel good about yourself, you'll still have the same feelings as everyone else—fear, anger, hurt, and so on—but because you know you're basically a wonderful person, such negative feelings will not affect you quite so deeply.

Isabel makes a brilliant decision—she pledges not to date for a year or until she feels better. The thought of twelve months without male diversion makes her faint with excitement. Usually she rebels at restrictions, but this one she chooses. Like a Girl Scout promising to do her best, on her honor she promises to make it on her own. It's official. She's the head of her household and not dating.

A sabbatical from dating is often a sensible choice. It prevents us from getting hooked up on the rebound. When we're vulnerable and needy, we need rejuvenating downtime. A dating sabbatical doesn't mean that we have to sit home. It simply means we're choosing to take a timeout. Without the tension of dating, we can take care of ourselves and relax. A dating sabbatical gives us a break from the pull of others so that we can focus on our own potential. Like a change of scenery, a sabbatical is rejuvenating. We can always start fresh when we want to.

try this

1. Consider whether you might benefit from a dating sabbatical. Trust your intuition on this one.

2. If the answer is yes, don't tell anyone yet. Try it on to see if it really fits, and keep it your secret until you feel comfortable with what you've decided.

3. Remember this is not written in stone; you can change your mind at any moment.

4. Go shopping for a journal, and buy yourself one that you really like. Write down your sabbatical goals.

5. Write the phrase: "An Exquisitely Wonderful Human Being" on the first page of your journal. Watch out! This powerful description will have a magical influence on the person who writes it.

> If you aren't good at loving yourself, you will have a difficult time loving anyone, since you'll resent the time and energy you give another person that you aren't even giving to yourself.
>
> —BARBARA DE ANGELIS

All Hearts Are Lonely

There are many people who truly like their single lives. They're happy, excited, and upbeat. They go through the day feeling optimistic and cheerful. They look forward to the weekend. Their schedules are filled with friends, family, and social activities. They know how to take care of themselves. They're independent and enjoy it. They're doing very well, but still, from time to time, they feel lonely.

Loneliness comes in degrees, from a mild "Whom shall I call tonight?" to a deep "What's it all about?" longing. As a single, you'll go through periods of not only feeling lonely, but of actually being alone. Your best friend is out of town, your buddies have gone skiing, the guy you met last week who said "Let's get together" hasn't called yet. You've called all your acquaintances and they're all busy. Now what! You don't have one soul to spend the weekend with. Ryan said it this way: "What I needed to hear when I was lonely was, 'Yeah, I know it's tough to be on your own,' but what people told me was, 'Oh, you'll find someone.' How in the heck would they know, they'd never been in my position."

> **"It's a bitch to be lonely, but it's better than feeling lonesome sleeping next to someone you barely know."**

Loneliness is a painful feeling. It's a gnarly beast that lurks around, smothers your delight, and leaves you standing sad and small. Leigh said, "On my worst days, I feel worse than lonely, I feel stale, abandoned, and forced by whims of fate to live alone. I feel very, very sorry for myself." Luke put it another way. "It's a bitch to be lonely, but it's better than feeling lonesome sleeping next to someone you barely know."

There are three layers of loneliness: social, emotional, and spiritual. We need to cope with all three. When we face the starkness of only being greeted by the dog day after day, it's depressing. When our answering machine is filled with more solicitations than invitations, we start to feel like a social outcast. When there's no one to cuddle in the middle of the night, our abandonment issues pop up, torment us, and keep us from sleeping. When we wish with all our might that we could find a special someone, we begin to wonder what's wrong with us. When our social calendar is filled, and we know that friends and family love us, but we *still* feel the ache of longing, we wonder where to turn. By identifying the layer we're grappling with, we're more likely to find a matching remedy. Conquering loneliness requires determination to get through the pain and curiosity to find out what's on the other side. Bette says that it's simpler being lonely on her own. "I can thrash about without the demand of my partner that I just get over it. When I have a bout of loneliness it might last all day. I usually get all my chores done, listen to music, and nap in the sun." Alicia told me, "Loneliness arises, and when it does I notice that it's there while I go about my day. Inevitably loneliness evaporates, and when it does I notice that it's gone."

When twenty-six-year-old Gracie moved from Denver to Chicago to take a new job, she didn't know one person. Although she was excited about her new responsibilities, she knew that she'd be lonesome. "I researched the city and developed anti-lonesome strategies. First I made a list of all the things that I wanted to see or do. Then I put the list on my bulletin board where I could read it every day. I wanted to be prepared because when I feel lonely I can't think and then I'm really stuck." Her list keeps her focused on learning about her neighborhood and the city rather than on how much she misses family and friends back home. Jared's strategy for social loneliness is to be active. After moving from Germany to Seattle, he joined a sailing club, a bicycling club, and took scuba-diving lessons. "It helps to see the same people every week."

To prepare your strategies, imagine all the things that you want to do. Imagine where you'd like to go, what you'd like to see, what you'd like to learn, and what kind of people you'd like to meet. Imagine being open to the surprises that will come your way, and imagine yourself feeling good. Do research, experiment, and try lots of new things. If something works, keep it on your list; if not, cross it off and move on.

For most of us, loneliness includes an element of existential longing. That's the need for connection to the Divine, to the mystery that flows through all life. Whatever strategies you're developing, be sure to include those that nurture the gentle tuggings of your soul. Perhaps singing in a gospel choir would fulfill that need in you, or perhaps, like me, sleeping under the stars soothes that blessed ache.

My daughter, Amanda, gave me a new perspective on loneliness when she moved by herself into a tiny apartment in the city. "Honey, won't you be lonely?" I asked. "Mom!" she reminded me, "I'm an only child, I like lonely." I hadn't quite viewed loneliness as something to like before she said that. I guess loneliness to me had been something bad, something to be avoided, to be pushed away with activities or distractions. But after she said, "I like lonely," I welcomed it.

try this

1. Prepare in advance for loneliness attacks by compiling a list of strategies for coping with the feeling.

2. Say to yourself, "Aha! Loneliness is arising." Watch loneliness come and go.

3. Do physical chores in threes to match the three layers of loneliness—social, emotional, and spiritual. Clean three closets, three drawers, three mirrors. Then vacuum the carpet, mop the floor, and empty the garbage.

4. Wrap yourself in a big blanket; lie down on a park bench and don't get up until you're good and ready.

5. Walk three miles, and if you still feel terrible, walk three more.

> At the innermost core of all loneliness is a deep and powerful yearning for union with one's lost self.
>
> —BRENDAN FRANCIS

Freedom Is Fun

Olivia is an independent lady. A dozen times each year, she gets up at 4:30 in the morning and goes scuba diving. At least that many times each year, she packs sack lunches, and around 8 P.M. she drives across town to hand them out to the homeless. Olivia is known to the regulars at the all-night diner as "that poet with the laptop in the corner booth." She's known to kids in the neighborhood as "the lady with the big garden, the one who will pay kids to pull weeds when the sun goes down." Olivia likes to do things backward. "I prefer to sleep in the middle of the day and stay up in the middle of the night."

Freedom is a big perk, the reward for being on your own.

George is a quirky guy. His weekly grocery list includes red jelly beans, portobello mushrooms, edamame beans, marinated tofu, organic strawberries, and carrots. He's happy that he doesn't have to consult with a partner about the food he buys.

Freedom is fun! In fact, the mystics have said that freedom is the ultimate, immensely valuable for personal and spiritual development. Perhaps it's because so much of our days are taken up with responsibilities at work and with obligations to our families that when a segment is free of those duties, it's pure exhilaration. There's so much bliss to be found in freedom.

Lydia loves being single. She wouldn't have it any other way, at least now. "When I'm part of a couple," she says, "My visions are squelched before they get off the launching pad."

Living freely is in part about defining our edges—getting acquainted with the you that's distinct and different from everyone else. Many couples crave that opportunity, too. That's because the lack of freedom kills spontaneity, dulls the senses, and turns what could be pleasure into mere routine. You've seen it, perhaps you've even lived through it, controlling pouty spouses fighting with each other. "How could you say that?" "Don't put that there." "You don't need that." "When are you coming home?" "You're late again!" "Where have you been?" "Do it this way." "Don't do that." Couples fight and compromise and resort to manipulating each other and by then, "The honeymoon is over."

Freedom is full of benefits. Singles can spread their wings and fly toward self-discovery. That's the way you get to know all sides of your personality. Singles are free from "shoulds" and "have to's" and "no, no's." You can paint the wall any color you choose, and paint it back again if you don't like it. You're free to be a walking contradiction and change your mind anytime. You're free to make yourself as happy as you want to be. You can buy an outlandishly expensive pair of shoes and not even hide them. You can move to your own rhythm. Leave the lights on and sleep on the couch, turn the lights off and read by candlelight. Move your bed into the living room.

The number-one benefit is the freedom to explore—without interference—a thousand and one ways to express yourself. In other words, you can express yourself freely—without interruption. Singles are free to choose what we want to choose without sifting through unsolicited suggestions.

Cherish your autonomy. It's such a delight to wake in the morning and bask in the wide-open space that greets you, such a treat to be able to explore all your options. If you've learned to roll around with freedom and appreciate the blessings that it offers, you'll bring a spark of "We don't have to be like other couples" to your lover, if and when you choose to have one. According to the teaching of the mystics, when love and freedom exist side by side, you've reached the highest peak.

try this

1. Be a walking contradiction and experiment by doing the opposite of what's expected.
2. Invite a friend to join you in the freedom of a moonlight stroll at midnight.
3. List the advantages of being single so that if someone should ask about it, they'll roll right off your tongue.
4. Be grateful for wide-open spaces in your day.
5. Throw your arms to the heavens and say, "Yes!"

When you give freedom to somebody, you have given
the greatest gift and love comes rushing towards you.

—OSHO

Take a Month for Crying Class

If you've ever listened to the slow, soft melody of a violin and a
classical guitar duet and felt an ache so deep that you wondered
if your heart might burst wide open . . . If you've ever stood
smiling in the midst of friendly men and women and felt a lump
in your throat so big that you couldn't speak . . . If you've ever
felt so abandoned by a friend that it took your breath away . . .
If ever you wonder whether you matter to anyone at all, then let
me assure you that you're on the right track.

Feeling a tug in your heart when you hear a sad story is
truly a blessing. Sadness puts us in touch with our sensitive side.
Alice likes to cry, and when she's hurt or deeply moved, she
weeps. "I feel better after I cry," she says. "That's why I like sad
movies. If I'm feeling down, but haven't been able to cry, I rent
a good tear-jerker and watch it."

Tears have many dimensions. There are the tears of pain
and suffering and the tears of happiness and delight. Tears can
signal that a heart is mending, wounds are healing, grief is
passing. That's what Adam, Lyle, Chloe, Linda, Danielle, and
Neil accomplished when they came together in a divorce
recovery group. Each felt out of place, like the lone person in a
world of couples, and each wanted to let go of the past and
have a fresh beginning.

It wasn't easy for six strangers to come together and share their troubles. It wasn't easy for Adam to talk about his wife's rejection. It wasn't easy for Lyle to admit that he hadn't been a very good husband. It wasn't easy for Chloe to stop judging the others as losers. It wasn't easy to be vulnerable in the face of judgments. It wasn't easy to stop blaming and pointing the finger. It wasn't easy to get over being mad. It wasn't easy to cry and feel helpless.

But since closing off and withdrawing didn't bring much happiness either, each took a chance and revealed their inner-most secrets. One by one they told their stories, cried, and were refreshed. "It's easier to let go of my husband," Danielle says, "than it is to let go of my fancy, married lifestyle." They laugh and grow more compassionate for themselves and each other.

When we don't express our sadness, we keep others at an emotional arm's length. When we're silent, withdrawn, and moody, friends have to guess about what's going on. They might get the mistaken notion that we're not interested in them. But when we share our vulnerabilities, we strengthen the bond between us. Risking self-revelation is scary, but the reward is a more meaningful connection.

Each time you hear a choir that sends a shiver up your spine, and each time tears roll down your cheeks, you're enhancing your capacity to live fully. You're sensitive, and it shows.

Feeling deeply, being moved, and crying is oh so cleansing. Haven't you felt refreshed after a good cry? Like the rain freshens the air, a good cry clears our foggy thinking. Tears of sadness, when allowed to flow, make room for tears of joy.

try this

1. Don't be a scaredy cat—share what you're feeling. You'll enhance relationship satisfaction that way.
2. Rent a tear-jerker, and invite your friends over for popcorn and a good cry. Send invitations that read: "Crying gets rid of stress. Come cry, and improve your looks."
3. Buy a couple boxes of tissue. Put one in your house and one in your car. Carry a beautiful hanky in your purse. You can still look fabulous while you're wiping tears.
4. Memorize this line so that you can put others who aren't as experienced as you are in these matters at ease: "Don't worry, I'm all right, I'm just crying, it's natural."
5. Cry and be gentle with yourself.

> We all like sad stories. It's so nice to feel sad when you've nothing in particular to feel sad about.
>
> —ANNIE SULLIVAN

Surround Yourself with Romance

My client Emme is the cutest girl. She has dark brown curls and big brown eyes. She has perfected her style—slightly vintage with lots of pink. She looks great; she's smart and funny. She has sparkle in her eye and a little spring in her step that makes you wonder what she's up to. Everyone says she has a lot going for her, and she does. But here's the clincher—she broke up with her boyfriend the first of January. She knows it was the right decision, but Valentine's Day is just around the corner. She's dreading it. She's having a rough time because "No one will be giving me perfume or flowers this year." She's agitated.

My client Eric is the greatest guy. Not only is he a 6'2" hunk, he's sensitive, athletic, well read, and kind to boot. He's thirty-six years old and a divorced father of an adorable four-year-old daughter. The ladies go for him, they ask him out, they vie for his attention, but he's miserable. He pines for his ex and hasn't recovered from his broken heart. More often than not, he's skeptical about the possibilities of finding the right woman again. When he walks into my office, he takes a heart-shaped candy from the dish, reads it, and says, "Cupid has it in for me."

Many of my friends and clients have a rough time around Valentine's Day. I did too, until I discovered a secret that made February my favorite month. Now instead of being left out, I go all out.

The secret that I uncovered is this: Love doesn't have anything to do with anyone else. Love is not a relationship. Love is a state of being; it's the condition of our own heart. Once I discovered that gem I was ecstatic, and I took Valentine's Day into my own hands. For me, that means baking heart-shaped cookies, buying expensive chocolate in gold-covered boxes, and sharing the goodies with anyone who walks through my front door. I celebrate with

Love doesn't have anything to do with anyone else. Love is not a relationship. Love is a state of being; it's the condition of our own heart.

as many friends as I can round up. Even if there is no knight in shining armor at my window, romance surrounds me.

I've started my own tradition, quite by accident. Years ago during the holiday season, I was quite depressed—so depressed that I couldn't muster the energy to send out Christmas cards. By February, however, the doldrums had lifted, and I wanted to reach out. I picked out frilly stationery and composed a letter, sending it out to everyone on my mailing list. The response was tremendous, and I simply had to keep the tradition alive! Except now I've extended it to last throughout the entire month. Every year, by February 1, I send out my annual Valentine's Day greeting. As I write, I sip the designated elixir for that month, sometimes vanilla lemondrops, sometimes Asti Spumanti. I adore writing the letter, and I adore hearing from out-of-town friends who, after reading it, pick up the phone and call. I adore that they look forward to my next one.

But that's not all. On February 1 of each year, I replace the white candles on the mantel in the sunroom and in my bedroom with good-smelling red and pink ones. They set a fanciful mood. I'm a sensuous lady, and I like my surroundings romantic. I keep plenty of logs for the fire on hand, and if I'm in the room, I keep it burning. Then I get the dining room table ready with my best china, napkin rings, and linens.

I fill every weekend of the month with celebrations for myself and for friends. I serve fancy drinks in stemmed goblets. One night the menu might be crab and cherry tarts, the next night lobster and chocolate-hazelnut torte, while another it's fondue and coconut pears. It's all deliciously decadent. My friend Jeff and I are both Aquarians, and we celebrate our birthdays together. I make French onion soup and he brings an ice-cream cake. The year that our combined birthdays added up to 100, he loaded it with candles and we blew them out together.

I buy myself dozens of red roses because I'm certain that all the men in my life—former and future—would want me to have them. I invite my girlfriends for lunch at Maximilian's in the Market to indulge in garlic-and-wine-drenched mussels and to drink as much red wine as we want. It's so much fun.

I give myself presents, too. This year, I'm giving myself a whimsical pink-velvet quilt that I've been lusting over since I saw it at Pottery Barn for Kids.

No, love and romance doesn't depend on anyone else. Some of my coupled girlfriends refuse to follow my advice. They resist the need to take action for themselves, and they pout or nag instead. They suffer from, "If he really loved me, he'd do such and such." They still abide by the notion that it's not romantic if I have to do it for myself. But not me! By the end of February, I'm satiated. I haven't had a moment for despair. I don't feel sorry for myself or think "Poor me." Actually, all through the love month, I'm purring. I'm always in love in February.

try this

1. Plan for Valentine's Day—and all holidays, for that matter—well in advance!
2. Buy Valentine's cards and mail them to every person that you know. I mean *everyone!*

3. Bake heart-shaped cookies—eat them and give them to your neighbors. If you don't feel like sharing, freeze a few and eat them in March.

4. Throw a cocktail party and invite a bunch of people.

5. Buy yourself something pink and wear it all month.

There are always more than two choices, always, always, always.

—PAT CALIFIA

Cinderella's My Role Model. Who's Yours?

My daughter, at age six, wanted as many versions of the Cinderella story as she could find. What's more, she read them eagerly. Even before she could read, she listened to them night after night on audiocassettes. When the movie was rereleased, we saw it together, loved it, and saw it a second time. Each time we left the theater smiling, singing, skipping, and happy. Originally I thought that the story of Cinderella was popular because Cinderella got her Prince Charming and lived happily ever after. I felt a little uncomfortable about it, a little embarrassed. I felt as though some dark hidden accuser were pointing a finger at me and disapprovingly saying, "Unrealistic!" Was I sending the wrong message by liking fairy tales with easy solutions? I certainly didn't want my daughter to have the idea that she could sit around waiting for Prince Charming. I think it's important to be self-reliant.

About the same time that we were reading Cinderella, there were books and articles published about the Cinderella complex, which warned women of the dangerous pitfalls of losing your independence and building your life around a man. I wondered: Is Cinderella really spreading the "You have to have a man to be happy" myth that so many women have been struggling to overcome? Does the story promote the idea that if you find a rich and handsome man, the rest of your life will be perfect? I wondered why the story of Cinderella was so appealing, and I also wondered why I felt awkward about it. So I decided to explore this further.

I asked Amanda, "What do you like so much about Cinderella?" Amanda usually has a lot to say, and she says it with a delightfully innocent wisdom, but this time all I could get out of her was, "I don't know, Mom, I just like it!"

Cinderella really gets a bum rap from some of her critics. These critics may say all Cinderella did was wait around for Prince Charming, that she simply let her fairy godmother perform the magic. They say that doesn't happen in real life. So of course they don't like their kids reading the darned book. Why? Are they so afraid their offspring might start living in Never Never Land and learn to avoid responsibility? They fear their children might get the idea that there's a fairy godmother somewhere or an enchanted prince who will always come along to kneel at their feet, bail them out, and rescue them. But take a closer look. That's not what happened in the story of Cinderella.

I think I know why Cinderella got her prince. When I looked closer, I found that the message my daughter was getting was really very positive. Cinderella has a cheerful spirit. Even though she's scrubbing and cleaning, she is vibrant. She makes the most of a deplorable situation. And look at the stepsisters—what are they like? They have everything, but still they're cranky and conniving, always complaining, fighting with each other, and jealous. Are these the qualities that anyone would want to be around?

Those stepsisters are always scheming. They're always planning their futures and plotting. They're jealous of each other, disgruntled. And what is Cinderella doing? She's singing and making friends with the animals! Oh, sometimes she gets sad and lonely, but somehow she is able to look at the bright side. When her stepmother tells her she can go to the ball, she eagerly and cheerfully sews a dress. Then, when Cinderella is about to go to the ball, the stepsisters in a jealous rage tear her dress so she can't go. The stepsisters go off to the ball, and Cinderella, sad and discouraged, goes out into the forest and cries.

Once again, Cinderella makes the most of an unhappy situation. Her friends the animals came to comfort her and what's more, she lets them. She doesn't try to hide her tears, she doesn't try to be strong—she simply cries. She allows herself to be natural. And when the fairy godmother appears, Cinderella is surprised, delighted, and full of wonder. She is open, eager to meet this strange-looking woman. The magic of the moment is not in the changing of the pumpkin to coach, but rather in the fact that Cinderella simply allows the fairy godmother to help her. She knows she couldn't do it on her own, and she allows the fairy godmother to give her a hand—that is the magic! Aren't those delightful qualities?

Cinderella's eyes are full of wonder when she arrives at the ball. But when the stepsisters arrive, their eyes are full of envy.

They didn't see how beautiful it all is. Instead, they immediately start plotting.

Cinderella lives happily ever after, not because she finds a prince to take care of her (although I'm sure that having a prince was a wonderful addition to her life)—she lives happily ever after because of who she is. And who is she? She's a person who knows how to make the most out of a situation she doesn't like. And she is a person who knows how to accept magic. She doesn't question or doubt the magic—what would she gain by that? She knows that miracles are part of life, which indeed they are. Miracles happen every day, and life is full of magic. Plotting and scheming and conniving, like the stepsisters do, makes life less enjoyable. It makes life drudgery and hard work, and then people become depressed and hopeless.

We're all a little like Cinderella. Perhaps you're working very hard; perhaps you're treated unfairly. Sometimes you might feel all alone. The story of Cinderella reminds us to believe in magic and miracles. It reminds us that hard work can be pleasant and rewarding. Cinderella reminds us that there is comfort in making friends with nature, and that there probably really is a fairy godmother watching over us. Finally, Cinderella reminds us that regardless of our circumstances, we can live happily ever after, even if there are setbacks along the way.

Finally, Cinderella reminds us that regardless of our circumstances, we can live happily ever after, even if there are setbacks along the way.

I think people live happily ever after because of how they live each moment. I think miracles do happen that can completely turn one's life around, and it's good to be open to the little miracles that happen in our lives. The stepsisters tried so hard to make their life different. It's as though they were in agony! Nobody wants to be around mean old stepsisters. I don't think they would have been open to a fairy godmother even if she had appeared.

Prince Charming has something to teach us, too. He didn't want just any woman; he only wanted the woman who fit the glass slipper. Almost fitting wouldn't do! And it never does. When I look around, I see that far too many people settle for less than what they want—out of fear that the right one can't be found, that the right house can't be found, that the right job can't be found, that the right relationship can't be found.

I remember a woman client of mine, Rachelle, a twenty-seven-year-old successful businesswoman who wanted to get married very badly. Because of her age, she felt she better find someone soon. So she gave up all hopes of ever finding her Prince Charming. One day a man she was dating asked her to get married. She said yes and set the wedding date. She really didn't love this man. One week before the wedding she was seriously considering calling it off, but she didn't. Her fear of never finding Prince Charming led her to marry someone she didn't want. After she got married, she called me and wanted to come for counseling with her husband, but he refused.

Cinderella didn't wait around for her Prince Charming. Oh, I'm sure she had dreams of him, and once in a while she thought of being rescued—that's perfectly normal. But her spirit is basically cheerful, and that's a role model we might want to know more about.

One more thing about Cinderella—she is a little mischievous! She makes a dress out of rags behind the stepmother's back. A little mischievousness lightens the spirit. Cinderella is assertive and creative. Cinderella is a real human being. She has dreams and hopes and fears and disappointments, and she probably gets angry, too. Some people think you can't be angry and also have a cheerful heart, but Cinderella proves that's not true.

The world is full of Cinderellas and Prince Charmings. All you have to do is open up your eyes and see. You may not have found yours yet, but be happy, and live each day with a little mischievousness, a lot of heart, and plenty of courage. There's nothing wrong with wanting to find your Prince Charming. Just be sure to embrace your inner Cinderella first.

try this

1. Let yourself believe in magic! Count the little miracles that float your way.
2. There is nothing to be ashamed about in wanting your Prince Charming, but don't let it become an obsession.
3. Take a trip to your local library or bookstore and read some fairy tales from your youth. I recommend "The Emperor's New Clothes" and "The Ugly Duckling." There are powerful messages in those stories.

4. Express your mischievous side in what you wear. Add a pink scarf, a big red flower, or go all out and make a dress out of the drapes.

5. Adopt a fairy godmother, and make it official. You need as many people working behind the scenes on your behalf as you can get.

My idea of superwoman is someone who scrubs her own floors.

—BETTE MIDLER

Chop Wood, Carry Water, Go to the Movies

"Okay," I said to myself, "if God is trying to teach me something, I'd better figure out what it is." It took about a year and two months after Jack had died before the shock of it all started wearing off. I was struggling to adjust to being single again and going through many changes. I couldn't predict the future, but my circumstances seemed to indicate that I would live a portion of my life without a man around the house. I didn't like the fact that God wanted me to be single, but that was my reality at the moment. Maybe God wanted me to learn how to take care of myself, how to manage on my own. I was a dependent personality who had to become independent—I didn't want to, I *had* to. Maybe that was by divine design.

The garbage disposal was the beginning of the quest. A daunting task. When the disposal clogged with potato peels, I sat on the kitchen floor and cried my eyes out. I felt relieved after that cry, but the disposal was still clogged. I called a plumber, but he couldn't come that day. (He was too expensive anyway.) Still moping, I read the instruction booklet, took the disposal apart, and put it back together. I had to jam it with a broom to get it moving, but it worked. God was happy, I could feel it.

When my car wouldn't start, I cried over that too. I was filled with grief and scared. I hated being on my own. I hated that there was no one to wipe my tears. I hated it that Jack's advice wasn't a phone call away. Life was so unfair, it really was. I knocked on the neighbor's door and asked Bruce—whom I'd never met—for suggestions. He pushed my car and got the battery started. The angels rejoiced at my initiative. I'd asked for help, and I'd graciously accepted what was given.

I wasn't fit for human companionship or small talk, but I needed to be around people. What should I do? Instantly a voice from the heavens spoke: "Go to the movies—alone." Learning the mechanical part of life management was easy compared to going to the movies. At twenty-nine, I'd never been to a movie by myself. It was fear, wrapped up with "What would people think?" Grudgingly I made a commitment to go to a matinee. That way I could sneak in without anyone's noticing. I was in for a shock. Outside the theater was a line of carefree, nonchalant, good-looking, laughing people—all couples—waiting to buy tickets. This is what they must mean when they say God works in mysterious ways. It was so easy for them. Why did God like them better than me? This was more than I'd bargained for. It would be impossible to sneak in without anyone seeing me. Standing by myself in line with strangers was not my idea of socializing. I could tell that they were thinking,

"Oh, the poor pitiful lady has no friends." I was mortified, but too depressed and too Christian to hate them. I hated being a lone person in a world of couples.

I wanted to wear a sign explaining that my husband had died. Except for walking the dog and going to work, I hadn't socialized for four months. Now I had to endure four minutes of torture to buy my ticket. Then I had to face another line to buy popcorn. The cheerful teenage girl behind the counter bugged me. I could tell she was thinking, "Why is this pitiful lady alone?" I shouldn't be expected to be polite or make new friends when I was grief-stricken. Doesn't she know I have friends who live out of state in California? Fortunately I'm a very stubborn person. I wasn't going to let her think badly of me. I was cheerful right back. "I'll have two small Cokes and two medium popcorns." There, I fooled her. I could hear the angels singing.

I don't know what made me think that traveling through Europe with a Eurail pass and backpack was a good idea. Perhaps it was because Jack and I had talked about going together, or perhaps it was a force beyond my control that drove me to it. In the back of my mind, I must have thought it would be good practice to be on my own where no one knew me. I arrived in Paris, caught the train to Amsterdam, found a hotel, and plopped myself down on the bed. Jet lag and terror at being alone in Europe stopped me from sleeping. I met two German guys in the lobby. They volunteered to take me to a club and on a tour of the red light district. I said yes, but wished that Jack were taking me instead. I compared the men to Jack. He was extraordinary, whereas these guys were average and not at all what I wanted. At four in the morning, I was sick of hanging around them, so I left them stoned in a bar. I'd walk home.

When you've been in a city for less than twenty-four hours, it's easy to get lost. When I started out, I thought I knew where I was going. I thought I would recognize my hotel. How many hotels have a brass knocker the size of a table at the entrance? Unfortunately for me, I didn't know the name of my hotel or its address. After wandering from canal to canal, it dawned on me that I was lost. I sat on the curb and cried. Jack would have known what to do. "Maybe if I sit here long enough, God will change his mind. This is a cruel joke, right? If you're the God of everything, do something now! Materialize Jack. Put him on this curb next to me this instant. I mean it!" It must not have been the kind of prayer that God answers because nothing happened. No Jack. No one noticed. No one asked me what was wrong.

It was up to me. I was clearly at a crossroads. I could become famous as the crying widow of Amsterdam, or I could find my hotel.

If anyone needed a miracle at that moment, I did. Maybe it was coincidence or some principle of quantum physics, because less than ten feet in front of me a big sign appeared that read "Youth Hostel: All Welcome." At the front desk, a polite English-speaking clerk made me a cup of tea and sympathized with my plight. "I'm staying at a hotel with an enormous brass knocker close to the train station and I don't know how to find my way back." "No problem," he said and called a taxi, told the driver the address, and bingo I was driven to the front door.

I didn't know it then, but I know it for certain now. Heartache is a very private matter. Grief stays with you until it's gone. No matter how hard I tried, I couldn't shake it. It clung to me like a fine layer of dust. Grief took up so much space. I slept with it, shopped with it, wined and dined it. It accompanied me through Rome, Venice, and London, and after three months I took it home. If there is a moral to the story, it's this: I can manage on my own better than I thought I could. I can read the instructions and fix a garbage disposal. If my car won't start, I can ask for assistance. If there's a movie that I want to see and no one will go with me, I can go alone. And when I go to Europe, I always write the address and phone number of my hotel on a piece of paper and carry it with me.

> Heartache is a very private matter. Grief stays with you until it's gone.

The Zen masters say that God is found in chopping wood and carrying water. That every tiny moment is as it should be. Life is not to be studied; it's to be lived. I agree with those Zen masters. Everything we need to learn, need to understand, or need to experience is right in front of our eyes, smack in the middle of our everyday, ordinary life.

try this

1. Grieve, and treat yourself to a new experience. It's true that grief takes time to lift, *and* it's also true that we might need to push ourselves a little as we adjust to being single. Start by reading the book *How to Survive the Loss of a Love,* by Peter McWilliams, Harold Bloomfield, and Melba Colgrove.

2. Pick one thing that you think might be good for you, and do it on your own. Practice by choosing something every week, and one of these days you'll be surprised at how much better the sense of accomplishment makes you feel.

3. If you've never gone to the movies alone—do it now! If you're sensitive about being around couples, try a matinee rather than an evening show.

4. Gather a toolbox with a cordless drill, a hammer, and a screwdriver. When things break down, check out the advice at *www.doityourself.com* or ask the neighbor for assistance. Take a class in auto maintenance. You don't have to do the maintenance, but understanding how a car works is helpful when talking to mechanics.

5. When out of town, always carry cab fare and the address where you're staying. If you get lost or confused, ask for directions.

> The hardest years in life are those between ten and seventy.
>
> —HELEN HAYES, SPOKEN WHEN SHE WAS EIGHTY-TWO

Reasons Not to Date

There are many reasons to get married and many reasons to stay single. There are good reasons to date and very good reasons not to. Thirty-nine-year-old Simone has an interesting spin on the dating scene. "Dating," she says, "comes with connotations associated with being a teenager." She doesn't use the term "dating." She prefers to focus on what she's doing. "I'm having dinner with someone, I'm meeting so and so for golf, I'm hanging out with the guy from the gym."

Simone made this shift to avoid the unnecessary pressures that come with dating. "As soon as you say you're dating someone," she says, "there are all kinds of expectations about what's going to happen next. Will he kiss me goodnight, should I invite him in, will he call me." For Simone, dating expectations get in the way of enjoying each other.

Some singles want to date, and that's perfectly natural. Others don't want to date at all, and that's perfectly natural, too. Some singles feel pressured to date. It's as if there's an unwritten code that implies that if you don't have a date on Friday night, you're a loser.

Let me assure you that you're not a loser if you're not dating. Many singles aren't dating—here are some of the reasons I collected from them:

- I don't want to be spanked or eat at McDonald's.
- He works for me and he has an alcohol problem.
- My boss kissed me and asked me out, but I don't believe in mixing business with pleasure unless I know that it's going to work out, and it never does, so why bother.
- I've given up dating young guys because I think they only like me for my looks and money.
- I make too much money and men are intimidated by my car.
- The older I get, the fewer men there are to choose from, and the fewer men there are that choose me.
- I don't own a computer.

- Women are always telling me I'm too nice or they're telling me about their old boyfriends. So I've stopped dating until the women grow up.
- Volleyball and dancing take up all my free time.
- I'm running a political campaign and just don't have the time right now.
- My girlfriend gets too jealous when I date.
- I'm too busy writing my book.
- Dating is for the youngsters; I only do dinner.

Dating is full of silliness, and single life is full of absurdities, the ridiculous, the ludicrous. There's never a dull moment when you're with singles. Whether you're dating or not, there are a thousand and one things to amuse you. It's a crazy world. I recently read a story in the *Seattle Times* about the sixty-eight-year-old woman who shot the seventy-nine-year-old man she was dating when she saw him talking and dancing with someone else.

My friend Jay says, "Dating is a little like sex. When you're having a lot of it you don't need it, but when you're having none it seems like desperate craving." To date or not to date, there's no right or wrong answer. Just when you decide you're never going to date again, your friends introduce you to someone cute, and you think, "Well, maybe."

try this

1. Make a list of the reasons that you're not dating. Ask your single friends their reasons.

2. Make a date at least every other week with yourself, and keep it. Take yourself somewhere special.

3. Write a poem about dating. Read Shel Silverstein or Judith Viorst and follow their style.

4. If you do decide to date, approach dating as if it's a party and you're the guest of honor.

5. Shh! Keep quiet! Don't flaunt how much fun singles are having, or everyone will want a divorce.

> I have only two kinds of days: happy and hysterically happy.
>
> —ALLEN J. LEFFERDINK

Singles Are in Style

The forms at Dr. Kilburns's office, my daughter's pediatrician, stumped me. What was my marital status? Technically I was no longer a widow, but at the time I didn't like the failure that I thought went with divorce. So I checked all the boxes: single, married, widowed, divorced. Then I numbered them in order, with single first, married second, widowed third, married fourth, divorced fifth, and single sixth. Then I wrote, "I can explain." I don't remember if he asked about it or not, but it must have been okay because over the years he sent me numerous clients. It was a small awakening. I would no longer label myself by my marital status. "No," I said to myself, "I won't be defined by the man I don't have."

It's a new day for singles. It wasn't that long ago that a single woman feared being a spinster at twenty-five. A man who didn't get married was either a shallow bachelor who couldn't settle down or a dirty old man. Fortunately, it's an ever-changing world, and singleness is no longer defined by stodgy standards. Today it would be difficult to find singles who fit those images. You're not over the hill at twenty-nine—you're a bachelor or bachelorette. You're no longer out-of-date at fifty; you're erudite and mysterious. You're no longer dismissed as a silly gadabout because you don't have a partner; you're idolized as sophisticated and worldly.

Singleness is an important rite of passage—a maturity maker—and those of us who grow through it have the pleasure and privilege of naturally ripening. Character is molded by self-reliance. "I'm learning what I value and who I am by making my own decisions," says twenty-four-year-old Karyn. "I'm not ready to settle down. I want to discover what excites me."

Character is molded by self-reliance.

"My single friends have been through hard times, and through it they've become wiser and sweeter. They're developed as individuals, which makes them more stimulating to be around," says forty-four-year-old widowed Illene. "I hate to say it, but my single friends are more active and well rounded."

Today's singles don't always view marriage as the ultimate goal. "I'd like to share my life with a special person someday, but right now I'm happy being on my own. I'm taking an art course in Barcelona next year, and I'm not sure I'd have that option if I was focusing on a boyfriend," says Joelie. Modern singles are relaxed about finding the right partner, because they know that fulfillment comes in many ways. They recognize the value of developing their own interests and pursuing their dreams. When they hit a rough spot—which of course everyone does—they find strength and abilities that they might not have developed if they could have automatically turned to a partner. Getting through rough spots builds resilience, a skill that serves singles well.

While it's true that singles sometimes envy the security of married life, it's equally true that couples sigh longingly for autonomy. "My married girlfriends sometimes tell me that they envy my interesting life," thirty-year-old Cameron says, "and I understand why. My options are open ended, while my married friends' futures seem set, as if the direction they're heading is established. I'm in the process of forging mine."

Singles are in style! We're all living longer, and we all can partake in as many different lifestyle choices as we choose. Singles are forging new territory—they're demonstrating that regardless of your age, regardless of whether you're a first-time single or single for the second or third time, you are on the cutting edge of inventing new ways of being in the world. Singles are not ashamed. They're not in hiding or holding back. Instead, they're involved and empowered. Singles can go anywhere

Singles are in style! Singles are not ashamed—they're involved and empowered.

and do anything. They don't have to wait. The single experience today is as full of the unexpected as any other lifestyle choice. Hurray for us! Singles today are respected for their courage, their vibrancy, and their ingenuity.

try this

1. Don't check the marital status box on all those forms! Cross out the boxes and write, "Stylish Single."

2. Be a good role model by honoring your limitations and celebrating your strengths.

3. Take a survey. Find out how many singles have chosen to remain single. Remaining single is a wise choice, and it's not a permanent condition.

4. Send accolades to your single friends. Aren't you glad you have them? Tell them how they've inspired you, how they make you laugh, and how grateful you are to know them.

5. Look around. Can you tell by looking who is happily single?

> I don't think there are prerequisites for happiness. I don't feel like I won't have happiness in my life unless I find a mate or unless I have a family. If I'm blessed with those things, then great. But I don't really have a list of things that I require in order to feel complete.
>
> —RENE ZELLWEGER

Quiz: Stuck in Single Stigma?

Take this self-scoring quiz to find out what beliefs are keeping you from being the best single you can be.

1. When I wake up in the morning, I pull the covers over my head and feel depressed at the thought of getting up.

2. I feel as if there is no one that I can tell my troubles to.

3. When I walk into a room full of people, my first thought is either "No one here is interested in me" or "There is no one here that I'm interested in."
4. I worry that I've said the wrong thing.
5. I worry about what other people think when they see me alone.
6. I feel like a total outcast going to the movies or dinner alone. It's better to stay home.
7. It is not natural to be single.
8. I can't enjoy life until I find my one true partner.
9. I should be happy without working at it.
10. When I see couples holding hands, I feel envious.
11. I feel like a total failure going to an event where everyone is single.
12. I would never go to a singles event because everyone there is a loser.
13. When I meet a man or a woman, I think of them in terms of their relationship potential. If they aren't relationship material, I ignore them completely.
14. Strangers are not worth talking to. Unless we're introduced in the right circumstances, there's no point in getting to know anyone. They won't like me, or I won't like them anyway.
15. I don't like small talk, and I hate parties.
16. Desirable, attractive people get married when they're young, and they stay together.
17. Meeting people is not fun at all; I'd rather stay home and read a book.
18. It is impossible to have friends of the opposite sex.
19. It is better to pretend that I'm not interested in romance.

20. I don't think I'll ever be happy alone.
21. You're selfish if you're single.
22. If you're not married by the age of _____ (fill in the blank), you're over the hill.
23. If you're young and single, you're on the make.
24. If you're old and single, you're lonely.
25. If you're single, it's because you can't settle down.

Scoring

Add up your total number of "true" answers, and read below what you can do next.

0–5   You've mastered the art of living single! You know that what you make of your life is up to you. You've overcome the single stigma and have risen above the crowd. Now you can go anywhere and do anything. You measure your worth not by whom you're dating, but rather by who you are. Your independence is appealing to others.

5–10   You're almost there! You're no longer ashamed of being single, and with that acceptance your attitude is turning positive. By facing singleness squarely, you're taking responsibility for your own happiness. Even though you may not always like being single, you're not going to let your marital status stop you from having a fabulous life.

10–15 You've come a long way, but you're still slightly ambivalent. You're holding on to the hope that if two needy people hook up, they'll make a whole. But that's not the correct formula. One needy person plus one needy person equals two needy people. A relationship goes smoother when one whole person meets another whole person. It's time to move from thinking that you need someone to feel complete. Keep working on your limiting ideas, and don't give up on yourself.

15–20 You're paralyzed by inaction and dependence on others. You're stuck with the stereotypical notion that it's terrible to be single. You have a lot of work to do to change that needy attitude. If you don't do anything, you'll stay clingy, and that's not attractive. Growing up is painful, but the rewards are big. Begin today by listing five positive characteristics about yourself.

20–25 You're ashamed of being single, and that's a heavy burden to carry around. No wonder nothing positive is happening for you! By answering this quiz honestly, you've taken a good first step toward making single life better. Let the stories in this book lift you up—you'll find singles who are making great strides. Follow the tips, and then take the quiz again. It takes work to be happy and independent, but it's definitely worth it.

3

Rising to the Occasion

Life takes many unexpected turns for all of us, but with a little gumption and determination, with a little guidance and good luck, we can take hold of our destiny. Single life is full of challenges—from breaking up, to living alone, to dating, to supporting ourselves—and it's full of many successes, thrills, and highlights. We can act as if we're not afraid, hold our heads up high, and pretend until we master the challenge. We can rise above our tendency to settle for less. We can learn, ask for help, and accept it. We can grow up, stand up, and seize the day. Whatever is happening, we can handle it.

Courting Rejection

Twenty-six-year-old Leigh hasn't had a date in seven months. Thirty-six-year-old Anna hasn't had a date in four years. Forty-three-year-old Jim says it's been a couple of years since he's asked anyone out, and he can't remember the last time a woman suggested that they get together. These three, like thousands of other singles, would like to have more dating opportunities, but they're not sure how to go about it.

Joe says, "All the girls that I like have boyfriends." Ingrid says, "All the good guys are married." Spreading the rumor that "All the good ones are taken" doesn't get any of us very far. In a way, it's an excuse that keeps us from doing anything about our situation. We either take action to get what we want, or we can make an excuse for not having what we want. We have to make a choice between taking action and making an excuse. It's impossible to do both.

The good news is that most people wish that more people would approach them more often. Single women wish that more single men would approach them. Single men wish that more single women would give them a clear indication that they'd like to be approached.

So what keeps us from reaching out to each other? Perhaps it's the fear of rejection. We don't want to make ourselves look foolish. What if we approach them and they say, "Oh, you old codger, leave me alone." That fear kept Kevin from calling Mary for more than six months. That fear kept Mary secretly wishing that Kevin would call.

If we want to reach out or approach someone, we have to get over our fear of rejection. In other words, we have to learn not to feel bad or be devastated when someone turns us down. We have to bounce back and court rejection.

If we want to have new people in our life, we should remember that the more rejections we get, the closer we are to winning the jackpot. There will probably be a sting. We may feel like crying or even get a little blue—we could even be mad as hell, and that's all right. It's okay to cry and be angry, but it's not okay to beat ourselves up. It is not okay to feel that we're a rotten, lousy person. We will be rejected, but we can't arrive at success without overcoming our fear of it.

try this

1. Say this phrase over and over and over: "I won't let a chance like this go by."

2. Instead of making excuses, take action. Draw a line down the middle of a sheet of paper. On one side, write the excuses you have for not approaching others. On the other side, write the corresponding action that is needed to turn that fear around.

3. Find something else to keep you company until you get over the sting of rejection. Go to a baseball game, hang with the books at the library, go for a bike ride, or volunteer to read to children.

4. Memorize the words to this song: "Somebody loves me, I wonder who, maybe it's you." Sing it in the shower, and let it be a reminder that seeking love is universal.

5. Bounce back. When you're feeling rejected, dejected, squashed, squelched, deceived, ignored, betrayed, and stomped on, cry and curse if it makes you feel better. Then start again.

> Life shrinks and expands in proportion to one's courage.
>
> —Anaïs Nin

The Thrill of Flirting

Flirting is great fun! It's a way to be playful, a way to bring new people—both men and women—into your life. Flirting is natural, a simple and tantalizing advantage of being single. Peacocks strut, birds flutter, singles flirt. It's intrinsic.

Everybody has a flirting style, but people go about it differently. Some are brazen and bold. They make flirting obvious.

Others are shy and coy. Some singles use the sly, seductive approach. Even listening intently to what another person is saying can be flirtatious. The dictionary says flirting is "to behave amorously without serious intent." Flirting is not serious at all. Flirting is simply letting another person know that you're interested in being playful. It's a fun way to let someone know you're interested. It's not necessarily about romance or sex. It's a way to get a friendship started—it's sort of the groundbreaking, a little bridge from you to them.

Some singles say they don't know how to flirt, but I think it's just that they're out of practice. With a little encouragement, everyone can do it. Anyone, that is, who isn't too solemn. If you've been brooding, depressed, or cranky, if you've lost your enthusiasm and can't find the zest for living, then you must flirt and be quick about it. Here are two rules to get you started:

1. Only flirt with people who flirt back. Remember that flirting is a way that two singles let each other know they're interested in being playful. If someone doesn't flirt back, they're probably not in the mood for fun. Flirting with someone who doesn't flirt back is a waste of time. Stop, and move on to someone else.

2. Just because you're flirting doesn't mean you have to "go all the way." You can stop at any time. You can flirt and have a good time with someone, and you can stop at any time. Flirting is thrilling, but it's not a commitment.

Think of it this way. Have you even seen a baby play peek-a-boo? First they get your attention. They get you to look at them. Then they cover their face with their hands! Then they peek out to see if you're still looking. They giggle and smile and cover their face again with their little hands. If you'll keep looking at them, and you cover your face with your hands and peek out at them, the game can continue for quite a while. If you ignore the baby, they'll just find someone else who's more willing to play peek-a-boo. Flirting is sort of like that. It's like a little game of peek-a-boo. If you think of flirting and start to get scared, think of yourself as a baby *and* the other person as a baby—flirting is just peek-a-boo for adults.

> **Flirting is just peek-a-boo for adults.**

Flirtation, like an unexpected present, can help you through a rough day. You missed the bus, hit your knee on the swinging glass door, bounced your rent check, forgot to call your sister—again—and, to make matters worse, you spilled salad dressing on the silk blouse you borrowed from her last week. Then, right out of the blue, a voice slightly behind your left ear says, "How's it going?" He says it in such a way that you know he isn't asking for details about your awful day. Is it the dimple or the strands of hair falling down his forehead that take your breath away? "Oh! Hi," you say, and suddenly you're batting your eyelashes and smiling. That's the way flirting works.

try this

1. Play peek-a-boo. Is there someone you'd like to flirt with but haven't had the nerve? When was the last time you flirted? Was it today, yesterday, last week, this month, this year, or so long ago that you can't remember? I suggest you stop denying yourself and treat yourself today.

2. Look directly at a friendly looking stranger. Smile, and say, "Good morning." Or say, "How's it going?" Linger long enough to hear the answer. Don't say it and run away too quickly.

3. Make eye contact. That's right, eye contact. Eye contact is very important. People across crowded rooms have gotten off their chairs to meet one another because of eye contact. I know because it happened to me once. Practice it a dozen times or more, and you'll know what I mean.

4. Practice this rhythm. When meeting someone new, don't stare off into space or at the floor. Look at the person you're meeting. Look right into their eyes, and then look away.

5. Loosen up. Let yourself go, and have a little fun! Don't be so standoffish.

> Love is so much better when you're not married.
>
> —MARIA CALLAS

Zen Dating

If you were twenty years old the last time you went on a date, you might be surprised to find out that even though times have changed, your feelings about dating haven't. Whether we're thirty or sixty, we still feel nervous and want to make a good impression. Dating is butterflies in the tummy, sweaty palms, and shaky knees. It's nerve-racking.

Dating will turn you into a sniveling neurotic faster than any amount of inadequate parenting. Jane was a fully functioning adult on Monday morning, but by Wednesday afternoon she'd reverted back to her trembling adolescent self. John, the guy she met at the coffee shop, the one she hoped would call, the one that she decided probably wouldn't call, rang her up. "How about taking a walk and getting a bite to eat?" Now Jane, who skillfully negotiates fifty-page contracts, goes into a frenzy and can't think. Or rather, she thinks too much. After that two-minute conversation, she couldn't communicate—not in coherent sentences, that is. "Oh my!" "Guess who called?" "Can you believe it?" "What shall I wear?" "What shall I talk about?" "What if I can't think of anything clever?" "What do you think?" "Do you think he'll like me?'

The Zen master hands out koans—What's the sound of one hand clapping? —to ponder. Dating koans—Whom shall I date? Where will I find him? Will she like me? —are equally baffling.

Dating is more about soul-searching and pattern-breaking than anything else. It's about getting honest and being vulnerable. In dating, we learn about who we really are, as opposed to who we think we are or ought to be. It's astonishing what we can learn by just thinking about dating. That's what makes dating very Zen. You know how the wise

Zen master presents the student with an impossible situation so that the student will learn about himself. The Zen master hands out koans—What's the sound of one hand clapping?—to ponder. Dating koans—Whom shall I date? Where will I find him? Will she like me?—are equally baffling.

Dating is full of self-evaluation, and every person we date teaches us at least one thing—even if it's something quite simple. Margo says she's eternally grateful that one of her dates taught her that the fastest way through downtown is through the slowest lane. Harry said he learned that he can't be poor if he wants to date rich women. Lydia learned that she's very intolerant of men who won't do the dishes. Uma says, "I tell myself it doesn't matter if he calls me again. I tell myself he's just one guy. I tell myself that if it's meant to be it will work out. I tell myself all kinds of things. Things that I know are true and yet I find myself waiting for the phone to ring and pining."

Megan learned about herself, too. First, she perfected attracting and pleasing. That was because she was more concerned with being liked than with whether she was doing the liking. She edited her opinions to agree with those of her date. After countless disappointments, Megan caught on and changed her behavior. "Instead of going out of my way to be what I think he wants me to be, I try to present who I really am. Now instead of thinking, 'Does he like me,' I think 'Do I like him?'"

Think of each date as a Zen master who can teach you a little something. Then instead of evaluating each date in terms of success or failure, you can reflect on what you've learned. Even if the two of you aren't clicking, welcome the experience and know that this person has learned from you, too. If we approach dating as a Zen practice we're energized and can enjoy the adventure.

try this

1. Instead of working at dating, work at being yourself while dating.

2. At the end of the date ask yourself, "What is one thing I've learned by spending time with this person?" Be thankful for that.

3. On your date, be sure to wear something that matches your mood. If you're not feeling cute, don't wear cute.

4. Follow the third date rule. Only make third dates with people who lift you up and bring out the best in you.

5. Remember, whether it's a frog or a prince you choose to love, the magic lies in you.

You meet someone new and it's a continual surprise.

—JAY SCHLECHTER

Let Them Down Easy

Breakups are not easy. No one likes them. Whether we've been seeing someone exclusively or only for a short time, parting without dumping is always the goal.

Joan wanted to let the man she'd dated four times down easy. She appreciated his intelligence and conversation, but there was no chemistry. She didn't want to hurt him, but she didn't want to lead him on.

After one year of seeing each other exclusively, Dan and Lia broke up. Thirty-four-year-old Dan was ready to settle down, but twenty-five-year-old Lia wasn't. She wanted to be on her own, to travel, to explore, to see more of the world. Dan's small business required that he stay put.

Dan and Lia cared deeply about each other, but they had to come to terms with the fact that they were at different stages in life. They liked each other, and they felt sad going their separate ways. They wanted to part peacefully, without trashing each other.

Even among the most civilized, breaking up often brings out our nasty, desperate side. "It's shocking to see how easy it is to slip into blaming," Ruby said. "When I was young, I didn't handle breakups very well. Since then I've learned that it feels so bad to hate someone you once cared about." Sam said, "If I'm shown the door, I behave like a gentleman. I'd rather be magnanimous than get caught in pleading."

When a love affair ends, we tend to think the love wasn't real. He or she didn't really love us. Otherwise, wouldn't they have stayed the course? Wouldn't it have lasted? But that's fallacious thinking. Everything that's vital sooner or later dies—that's the very law of life. "In the middle of our break, I met my soon-to-be-ex for coffee, and I could feel what it feels like to be done with a person. He was the father of my child and I wanted to treat him respectfully," Loretta said.

Breaking up with dignity is honoring the person whom we once loved while we go our separate ways. Don't expect to do it perfectly, but try to do your best.

Any person who comes into our lives comes in to teach us something. Even if they've given us something that we now know we don't want, that's still a worthwhile lesson. There's something positive to learn from all relationships, even those that caused us pain and suffering.

A satisfied single knows that each breakup is an opportunity to be gracious. We can behave in a calm, nonjudgmental manner. We can be honest, clear, and direct, or we can hint by not answering the phone and by giving double messages. There are so many ways we can disagree, find faults, blame, and point fingers that we often get sidetracked and embroiled in a myriad of reasons. Keeping the explanations simple—"I appreciated the time we spent together, but this is not a match for me"—will keep you from getting lost in analyzing.

> Once a person has had a place in your heart, you can't throw them out. They're in your heart forever. That doesn't mean that you have to live with them, sleep with them, or invite them over.

A satisfied single would never put the dread of confrontation ahead of telling the truth and clearing the air. Once a person has had a place in your heart, you can't throw them out. They will remain in your heart forever. That doesn't mean that you have to live with them, sleep with them, or even invite them over. A satisfied single is gentle toward this other person who, like you, took a chance. Such a satisfied single offers the hand of compassion even while parting.

try this

1. Commit to behaving like a lady or gentleman.
2. Put yourself in the other person's shoes. Ask yourself, "If this person were me, how would I want to be treated?" Tell them directly, "Our relationship isn't a match." Say it kindly so that they save face. Don't prolong the agony by hinting.
3. Be positive, be firm, and acknowledge what you learned.
4. Gather your friends and have a cry-fest. Work out your anger at the gym rather than on your ex.
5. Be grateful for what comes; be grateful for what goes.

> And never, never, no matter what else you do in your whole life, never sleep with anyone whose troubles are worse than your own.
>
> —NELSON ALGREN

Be Thoughtful About Where You Put Your Energy

When we live alone, we can keep ourselves company by having great conversations—conversations with ourselves. That's a blessing or a curse, depending on what we're talking about. We can have the same boring round-and-round discussion about regrets and "if onlys." We can complain about being over the hill and moan about being unloved, or we can contemplate the bigger issues. We can have a one-on-one chat about the existential questions, like "How can I live a meaningful, flourishing life? How can I thrive on my own? How can I have satisfying connections?"

When I suggested this in a presentation to a singles group, one young man objected, saying, "I'm not a philosopher." Several people nodded in agreement. "Okay," I said, "So you're not philosophers. Well then, perhaps you might consider what you're watching and what you're gossiping about." I'll give you an example of what I mean.

Twenty-seven-year-old Margaret is full of free-floating anxiety after the end of her brief marriage. During the day she's busy at work, but in the evenings she doesn't know what to do with herself. She's so accustomed to having a husband to distract her that on her own she's bored. "I'm not use to silence." With no noise to divert her attention, Margaret's jumpy. She's in transition and doesn't know how to handle it.

At the checkout counter, Margaret bought a paperback novel with Fabio on the cover, and that evening she absorbed herself in romance. It was the beginning of a nightly ritual. For months she's been swept away with fervent clinches and bulging biceps; she swoons over passionate embraces and heaving bosoms. Unfortunately, she's living vicariously through the heroine. At the end of 250 novels, she's lethargic and even more down in the dumps. And so is twenty-five-year-old Brad, a good-looking guy, who after working out at the gym spends his evenings conquering villains in the company of his Xbox. Thirty-six-year-old Allyson has watched *Out of Africa* and *Crossing Delancey* so many times that she's memorized the lines. Megan numbs herself too, only her drug of choice is gossiping on the phone with her sisters—about each other.

During transitions, it's sometimes best to give up familiar activities that keep us going in circles. When Candice is pining for an old lover, she stops watching romantic comedies because they feed her unrealistic ideas about not being desirable unless she's desired by a man. Creating a flourishing, balanced life and keeping your heart open is work, and we have to work hard at it. Sometimes we have to give up one thing to get another. Liza gave up gossiping about men. "Whenever my friends and I got together, I noticed our tendency to compare man stories. It was fun and even helpful, but I'd fallen into a rut of talking about myself in relationship to the men I was dating. I gave up gossiping about men to focus on my other needs. No more man-bashing or war stories for me."

> Creating a flourishing, balanced life and keeping your heart open is work, and we have to work hard at it. Sometimes we have to give up one thing to get another.

A robust life doesn't sprout from romantic novels, video games, chat rooms, gossiping, or hibernating in a safe cocoon. It grows from thoughtful options about where to put your energy. It comes by carefully choosing what you think about, what you watch, and where to go. It begins with considering what you want to do with the hours you have to spend on earth. Be careful where you put your attention. Be discriminating about what ideas you soak in. Romantic images have a subtle yet very potent power to influence us, and that may not always be in the interest of our highest good.

In a way, we're all incomplete souls searching for wholeness. Often, we turn toward numbing entertainment when we're feeling incomplete. Or we rely on one relationship as a way to feel complete. While that's natural, that's a heavy load for one friendship or one love relationship to deliver. All relationships fall short of filling us up. Romance, love, and companionship are ingredients of a wonderful life, but they're not the main ingredient or the only source of joy. We need both companionship and solitude. We need others and ourselves. We need time together and time alone. It's not one or the other—it's both.

> **All relationships fall short of filling us up. We need both companionship and solitude. We need others and ourselves. We need time together and time alone. It's not one or the other—it's both.**

try this

1. Inspire yourself. Don't feed your hunger for a love affair on a steady dose of romance novels or romantic movies. If you want to see a movie, get the book, *Cinematherapy: The Girl's Guide to Movies for Every Mood,* by Nancy Peske and Beverly West. Choose one that will elevate your thinking or clear up some unfinished business.

2. Have you been to the symphony? Dress up in a pretty outfit, and take yourself out. If you're worried about what people are thinking about you, they're probably thinking, "My, what a well-dressed woman."

3. Contemplate and gossip about the existential questions: How can I live a meaningful, flourishing life? How can I thrive on my own? How can I have satisfying connections?
4. Volunteer! Get off the couch and make a contribution. In the twenty-first century, meaning comes to those who are making a difference in the world.
5. Give up numbing habits that prevent you from making conscious choices.

> When I meet a man, I ask myself, 'Is this the man I want my children to spend their weekends with?'
> —RITA RUDNER

An Apartment for One and Cooking for Strangers

Katy lives alone in her "hideaway for one." She loves to throw parties—ordinary parties where friends drop in and raid the refrigerator and extraordinary theme-party bashes with invitations and catered food. You can learn a lot from watching thirty-seven-year-old Katy. She has gathered good people around her and made a cozy, contented home for one. It wasn't difficult for Katy to adjust to living alone after her divorce. "I prefer living alone, perhaps that's because I was an only child. I like my own space and I'm used to entertaining myself."

Katy's hideaway is comfy, but it's not conventional. In the winter, she sleeps on her combination day bed/couch in the living room right next to the fireplace. In the summer, she moves the bed through the French doors onto her patio. She turned her bedroom into a multipurpose room for yoga and sewing her one-of-a-kind wall hangings. The bedroom now serves as an office and party room for dancing. One February, her guests gathered around the worktable to make Valentines.

"I like living alone, but I don't like eating alone." That's how the party thing started. Katy didn't want to eat alone on Sunday nights anymore, so she invited a couple of friends for soup. After a while she encouraged friends to bring friends, and slowly it evolved into an open invitation for once-a-month Sunday Night Soup. Katy includes a variety of friendly strangers—from her mailman and the receptionist at the gym to her financial planner and the neighbors. "My dream is to one day start a communal, cooperative restaurant because I think eating together, sharing a meal and great conversations is one of the supreme pleasures in life."

Entertaining is Katy's lifeline. "It's impossible to be lonely when I'm absorbed with the ripeness and color of the tomatoes that I'm putting in the soup. Mix in lively gossip, and I'm in heaven."

Katy is a rich woman, rich with friendships. "It's the alliance that we all need to help us through all our other relationships."

> If you don't have a romance, that's annoying. But if you don't have friends, you're in big trouble.

She's right. There's too much emphasis on one-on-one relationships. It's as if a significant other is the only satisfying way to be cared for—it's not. If you don't have a romance, that's annoying. But if you don't have friends, you're in big trouble.

It's easy for Katy to get acquainted. She's instantly likable and inquisitive. She brings out the best in people. She makes everyone an insider. It's not as easy for Gavin. He's shy and hasn't recovered from the pain of his breakup. He's broke, paying off school loans, and his apartment only has one comfortable chair. But he has a lot to offer even when he's cranky. His most important quality is that he makes the effort and he's persistent. "I make friends doing what I always do—running." Gavin runs three miles around Greenlake every day. He formed the Run for Brunch Bunch to run around the lake together on Sunday mornings and go out for brunch. He never gives up on running or going to brunch, and he keeps asking people to join him—so often that they finally do.

The wonderful benefit about being single is that you can be open to all kinds of people without worrying that you're offending your spouse. You can give a dinner party for one or for as many as you like. You can invite couples or not. You can invite only men or only women. That's what Nicole did. One year she gave a girly party for girls only, and then the very next month she followed that up with a cigar-and-brandy party for "only the boys and me." "I really didn't know that many men, so I invited the four that I knew

If you live alone, you don't have to be alone. The secret of success is persistence.

and asked each of them to bring along another guy. My girlfriends were very jealous when the guys taught me how to play poker." If you live alone, you don't have to be alone—you can invite people over. If you can't cook, you can still have people come over. Ask them to bring the food. If you don't want to join an established club, you can start one of your own. The secret of success is persistence.

try this

1. Be a little bit avant garde, and sleep around the house. It will boost your energy to sleep in a different room each night.

2. Decorate your home to reflect the daring side of your personality. If you don't know what that might be, ask your friends to describe it for you.

3. Follow Katy's and Gavin's example, and be welcoming and persistent. Invite, invite, invite; reach out, reach out, reach out. Don't let a slow start dampen your resolve.

4. Start a club. I once started a club called the Gray-Beard Club. I put an ad in a local paper that read, "Open to all men and women who have a gray beard, know someone with a gray beard, or would like to." If you like this idea, go ahead and use it.

5. Be a warm and welcoming host. When people come to your home or event, be enthusiastic and show them that you are thrilled that they have come.

It's like magic. When you live by yourself, all your annoying habits are gone.

—ANONYMOUS

Support Yourself in Style

Supporting yourself in style isn't about getting rich—it isn't about buying designer clothes, expensive cars, or lavish homes. Supporting yourself in style is earning enough to pay your expenses, earning enough to save, and earning enough for treating yourself when you want to. Supporting yourself in style means doing work that has personal significance by using your talents and cultivating your interests.

Hank and Marla are both single and support themselves in style—although their notions of what "in style" means is very different. For Hank, it's a condo with a view, a fancy car, expensive clothes, picking up the tab at dinner, and flying first class. His medical-equipment sales position supports his tastes. He likes the pressure, and that's what he chooses. For Marla, supporting herself in style is a studio apartment, riding the bus instead of driving her twelve-year-old car, shopping consignment, taking sack lunches, and in-line skating. She has two part-time jobs: one teaching dance—"I couldn't live without dance"—and one as a barista at a coffee shop. She simplifies her finances by spending less, and that way she has more—more time for doing what she loves. For her, managing less stuff equals more free time.

The secret to supporting yourself in style is simple: Stop comparing yourself to everyone else. You need approval from no one but yourself. Just because Hank has a leather couch doesn't mean you have to own an expensive couch to live in style. Just because Marla prefers part-time jobs doesn't mean that's the only way to work.

How do you find your style of living? By experimenting. That's the fun of being single. Ed lives on his sailboat in a marina and works within biking distance of his office. Tim earns enough money fishing in Alaska to travel for three months during the off season. Traveling is both Quinn's work and her hobby. She's a travel photographer and takes stock photos for advertising. Imagine the kind of work you would find so rewarding that you'd do it for free. Imagine where you'd live if money weren't in the equation. Those are clues to where you'll find your true style of living. Supporting yourself in style requires hard choices as well. You may be able to get a high-paying job, but that might mean making a "not worth it" tradeoff. Some people work eighty hours a week and have a big paycheck, but they have no free time.

My friend Sophia traded in her corporate job for the oppor-tunity to teach writing workshops and to do some freelance editing. She wears big black horned-rimmed glasses and white flowing linen dresses. When she had a corporate job, she earned more money, but she had to wear suits, and for her, dressing that way wasn't worth it.

She's happily single and self-employed. Her life is full and her work exciting, even if she's not rolling in the dough. Whenever Sophia and I get discouraged—which we all do— about the cost of living and our personal economy, we remind each other that we have everything that's important and worth-while—friends, art, music, laughter, good health, the love of our children, and meaningful work. That's all we really need to be happy.

Consider this: Are you satisfied and fulfilled by your job? If not, is there one small change that you can make that would add more meaning to your work? You may not have the ideal job, but you may be able to make your work day more pleasant. Instead of pushing yourself and racing around to get more done, you can take a deep breath, slow down, and accomplish just as much. Perhaps you can make your work space more appealing by putting one long-stemmed rose on your desk. Instead of taking work so seriously, perhaps you can approach it playfully.

Supporting yourself in your own style is a goal worth thinking about. Even if you haven't accomplished that yet, planning for it is the first step toward achieving it. Remember—while it's easy to fret over lack of money, the lack of a good idea and creative work is the real obstacle. So here's to a year full of good ideas backed up by creative, hard-working genius. And for financial reasons of course, here's to a year full of prosperity.

try this

1. Ask yourself the question, "What do I need to be happy?" List your top three priorities.

2. Set personal goals that matter to you. Achieving goals that someone set for you isn't any fun at all.

3. Hang out with folks who have a similar lifestyle philosophy. When you're discouraged or being hard on yourself, you'll have a backup perspective and vice versa.

4. Reflect your style at work. Make two changes in how you do what you do in order to make your job resonate more closely with who you are. Make two changes in your work surroundings that give it a more personal touch.

5. Tired of stuff management? Want to simplify? Give the gift of re-gifting. Look around your house. I'm sure there's something perfectly lovely that you don't really need that would make a lovely gift. I always tell my friends, "This is a re-gift." They don't seem to mind—although they usually want to know the history of their new treasure.

> Hard work spotlights the character of people: some turn up their sleeves, some turn up their noses, and some don't turn up at all.
>
> —SAM EWIG

Earn Your Own Jingle

If you're supporting a family, yourself, or cat, here's to you! What an enormous achievement that is. It's not easy to get up every day and go to work. It takes considerable determination. If you've ever had to support yourself with no backup, and if you've ever had an unexpected expense with no one to rely on, you know what a huge task carrying the entire load can be. If you don't have enough money to get you through the end of the month, you've experienced how draining that worry is. If you have rent to pay, a mortgage, a car, insurance, loans, or children, you're all too familiar with unending expenses.

Elaine works two jobs to pay off college loans. Mary works two part-time jobs while she's applying for one in her field. Matt drives an hour and a half each way to his office so that he can live near his son. Rene's pay as a schoolteacher doesn't go far enough, but she prefers a work schedule that matches her kids'. To earn extra, she plays the piano for weddings and funerals, and takes the girls with her. Isn't it amazing what a single person can do?

There are so many expenses—a roof needs patching, the computer needs updating, the kid needs soccer shoes, the brakes on your old car are grinding. One paycheck is seldom enough to balance a budget. When the only person you can borrow money from is you, when the only person managing it all is you, when there's no on else to pitch in, it's stressful.

Financial pressures are a reality, and one of the most stressful burdens is not having enough to go around. If you don't have enough to pay the bills, that worry zaps your energy. So what do you do if you can't borrow from a bank, a rich uncle, or your parents? You learn to set priorities and say no. You go without, make do, and develop ingenuity. That's what five friends did. Paul, Victoria, Lee, Eda, and Jane formed a prosperity club through their church singles group to learn about investing, money management, and living simply—or, as they put it, "Simply Living." "I'm amused by what I'm achieving through scrimping," says Jane, who was in debt when she joined the group, but isn't now. "By defining my financial goals and sticking with my intention to get debt free, I've learned about making sound choices for myself." Monthly meetings keep them on track. "Talking about money is as personal as talking about sex," Paul told me. "In our group everything is confidential." To get in financial shape, they do financial exercises:

1. Talk about money and dependency issues.
2. Figure out what you need, and buy only necessities for a while.
3. Write a financial vision statement.
4. Keep an ongoing list of spending and saving priorities.
5. Share with the group.

With the support of "Simply Living," members have explored the resistance that comes up around money. Taking charge of one's own financial destiny is about being responsible. While many of us claim to want power and control over our money, we're resistant at the same time. We wish for someone else to do it all or take up the slack. Coming to grips with one's own childlike wish to have whatever we want without working or saving is required for mature independence. We have to give up wanting what we want when we want it and wanting someone else to give it to us. Our attitude toward money is a barometer for how vulnerable we're feeling. If we're dependent on someone else for making the money, then we don't have much power. Everyone needs the power that comes from jingle in their pockets.

> **Coming to grips with one's own childlike wish to have whatever we want without working or saving is required for mature independence. We have to give up our sense of entitlement.**

try this

1. Congratulations! If you're working, supporting yourself, and managing your money, please don't take this achievement for granted. Congratulations are in order. It's not easy, it's not always fun, and you're doing it.

2. Start a financial planning group for singles only. Call it "Sex and Money," and you'll probably attract lots of members.

3. Examine your attitude toward money. Is that childlike wish to have someone take care of you getting in the way of becoming financially responsible? Is the adolescent impulse to have what everyone else has causing you trouble?

4. Carry your own jingle. (Credit cards don't jingle.) Don't buy it unless you really love it. Go without until you can treat yourself by paying right up front.

5. Get acquainted with the evening. Take a second job, and work the late shift. You'll be so exhausted that you'll be able to fall asleep standing up and won't have time to spend money.

Money is better than poverty, if only for financial reasons.

—WOODY ALLEN

Humor Your Parents

When forty-six-year-old Leila broke up with Alec and he moved out, it left her living alone in the apartment they once shared. "You're not going to stay there?" her mother pleaded in a tone that let Leila know she didn't approve. "But there's no doorman in the building. Why don't you look up Todd? His mother told me that he lives less than a mile away in a very secure building." Which translated, means Mom wants daughter married and safe.

When eighty-six-year-old Olga moved in with her sixty-seven-year-old bachelorette daughter Mildred, it was one question after another: "You're staying out until 11:00 on a weeknight?" "Do you think it's proper to be seen with Fred so soon after his wife died?" "What are Fred's intentions?" "Mom, I'm sixty-seven," Mildred reminded her. "That is beside the point," Olga scolded.

Twenty-four-year-old Abigail, out of her five-year relationship for only five months, gets asked weekly by her anxious and slightly neurotic mother, "When do you think you'll get married again?"

It's the same for my fifty-two-year-old friend Anthony. He's never been married, although he's never lacked for female companionship—he prefers the single life. His motto is "Laugh and the world laughs with you, get married and you'll sleep alone." His mother doesn't think that's funny. She doesn't like him "sleeping around." She wants him safely married. She wants grandchildren. She wants him respectable and settled down before she dies. "That's the good thing about gray hair," Anthony told me. "My mother stopped fixing me up a couple of years ago, now she just rolls her eyes and sighs."

Aren't these mothers silly? But it's not just mothers. Brooke's father cross-examines any guy she brings around. He wants to make sure the guy comes from a respectable family, that his intentions are honorable, and that he has a good head on his shoulders. Brooke's dad likes a guy who can look him in the eye, shake his hand, and who is up to date on the stock market. If the guy fails any part of the test, Dad calls Brooke with assessments and recommendations. "He is not for you," he'll say.

It's no wonder singles feel so pressured when even parents are pushing matrimony.

If you've got parents, you're going to get questions and advice and disapproving glances. Answer them as sweetly as you can, smile and ignore the others. That's what Brooke does. "Yes, Dad, I see what you mean," she says and then changes the subject. Leila repeatedly gives reassuring pats on the shoulder along with, "I'm fine, Mom, really I am."

Questions from parents, like "Are you eating your vegetables?" or "Why do you need to buy a new car?" or "When are you going to settle down?" or "You're traveling alone to where?" are annoying, but understandable—after all, parents are parents.

You might be called on to do some parental reassuring too. You understand why. Your parents are desperately hoping to get you safely adopted—preferably by a combination millionaire, doctor, and gourmet cook—before they die. They need you to have a family so they can brag about their genius grandchild. They want to rest in peace knowing that the family genes are passed on and that you're safe and secure with a marriage certificate and a house. They don't want to be rolling over in their graves, frantic with guilt and worry about you.

Be patient. Logic won't work. They probably will never outgrow their ruminating, and you can't change them. It doesn't matter that you've reached a certain age or that you have plenty of options. What matters to them is that you're an SAC (single

You can bet your parents are contemplating where they went wrong, so please be pleasant.

adult child) who shows no signs of walking down the aisle. The older and more unmarried you get, the more they're fretting. You can bet your parents are contemplating where they went wrong, so please be pleasant.

Humor your parents. That's what Leila does. She moves away from logic and reasoning and simply humors her mother. "Yes, Mom, I am thinking about settling down." "Okay, I'll call Todd next week." "It's okay Mom, I'm eating healthy and yes I'm eating vegetables." "Mom, I'm fine." "Okay, I'll consider meeting your friend's nephew."

try this

1. Hush! Don't tell your parents everything, but do throw them an inside tidbit now and then. Otherwise they'll get overly anxious.

2. Smile and say, "Yes, Mom, I see what you mean" when she gives you dating advice. Give your dad a reassuring hug and kiss on the cheek when he hands out recommendations or assessments about the people you're seeing.

3. Humor your parents by nodding, distracting them, or changing the subject. When you can do this sweetly and kindly, it's an indication that you're beginning to grow up.

4. Don't argue with your parents. Lobbying about the benefits of single life won't change their minds, and they're likely to conclude that you're being disrespectful.

5. When all else fails, tell them you're considering becoming a monk or a nun.

I became a nun, because although I recognized it as having many ramifications . . . foreign to my temperament, still, given my completely negative feelings about marriage, it was the least disproportionate and most fitting thing I could do.

—JUANA INES DE LA CRUZ, CIRCA 1691

You're Never Really Alone

Often, as singles, we get so focused on finding someone to love us, that we rationalize that there really is no one to love. We tell ourselves, "No one cares about me" so many times that we start believing that it's true. We grow very self-centered doing that. Instead of loving others, we complain that no one loves us. We make dozens of excuses: "I hate small talk." "No one's interested." "No one's interesting." We shut down and close off. We become super-duper independent. We make justifications. We're too busy for chitchat. We're too intelligent for idle chatter. We excuse ourselves from taking any initiative to get to know others. We wait in our ivory tower for someone to approach us, and the ivory tower is a dangerous place to be. Slowly, loneliness turns into hostility. Our pride takes hold, and we've walled ourselves in so tightly that we grow bitter. We begin criticizing those around us.

The more we remain focused on our narcissistic selves, the more alone we become. Though it's difficult, reaching out is always preferable to closing down.

Rita, single for the second time, is a people magnet.
Everywhere she goes, she's making conversation. "Why do you
talk to so many strangers?" I asked. "Everyone is a stranger until
you talk to them," she told me, "that's what I like about them."
Rita likes to know what's going on. She likes to find out information. "You never know where one little chat might lead."

Rita uses small talk like a bridge. "I like your purse," or
"Where did you get those cute flip flops?" or "Oh, what a cute
dog," to get conversations started. "Strangers are my biggest
resource," she boasts.

Rita turns to people for entertainment: "People-watching is
better than movies"; for advice: "What do you think about my
hair cut?"; and for contacts: "I'm looking for a handyman, do
you know anyone?" She'll ask anyone, from the grocery clerk
or the lady at the Laundromat. "It never hurts to ask, and it
almost always leads to someone who knows someone who
knows someone who might." Rita's secret to meeting people is
that she talks to strangers and then she asks them about what
they might know. "Everyone likes to talk about themselves and
be helpful."

"Do you know anyone who needs a tennis partner?" she
asked the receptionist, while she was waiting for the doctor.
"I'm a beginner and need to practice." The receptionist didn't
know a tennis partner, but the conversation got going and
ended up with Rita getting the number of the receptionist's
friend who was in beauty school and needed models for the
cutting competition. Rita ended up with a free haircut, color,
and style from that one conversation. That's the way it happens.
Rita found her baby sitter from a cousin of a friend, her dog

from the librarian's mother, and her temporary job from a real estate agent who was listing the condo next door.

You might think that Rita talks to strangers because she's outgoing. While it's true that she's definitely not shy, it's really more than that. Rita trusts. She believes wholeheartedly that we need each other. "Tell enough people and it will be delivered," she says. "That's what the Bible means by, 'Seek and ye shall find' and 'Knock and the door shall be opened.'"

Rita likes strangers—she doesn't define them with a negative view. She's over "fear of outsiders" and won't allow "fear of rejection" to rule. When someone isn't friendly, she's unflappable. "It's okay, they're occupied."

You see, Rita loves loving, and it's a two-way street for her. Mention a need, and she's hooking you up with someone who does that very thing. "My bicycle chain is broken," I complained. "Call Mike, the bike guy, and tell him I sent you." It's a neighborly thing to do to reach out and help one another.

All the mystics tell us to be more loving. Love doesn't come from a "How can I get more for me?" attitude. Rather, it blossoms with "How can I give love to you?" Pursuing someone to *love us* is doomed; it's in loving others that we find love.

try this

1. Follow Rita's lead, and visit with strangers.
2. If you have a need, tell it; if you see a need, fill it.
3. Ask yourself: What can I do, what can I say, what can I give?

4. Use small-talk bridges—"I like that bracelet," "I like that shirt," or "What's that music you're playing?"—to get conversations going.

5. Share resources—your handyman, your baby sitter, your hairdresser, or any other resource that might be helpful.

If you're scared, just holler and you'll find it ain't so lonesome out there.

—JOE SUGDEN

Be in Love—With Life!

Thirty-four-year-old Tess is a beauty—long legs, flowing brown hair, high cheekbones, and wide-set blue eyes. She has good looks, a runway model attitude, and a haunting conviction that she's right—no matter what. Well, that's the way she acts when she's in love. When she's not in love, she slips quickly into negativity and turns slightly suicidal.

Tess likes falling in love. When she's in love, she's on top of the world and cocky. When she's not in love, she can barely get out of bed. After each breakup, she spends a month or more crying, smoking, and not eating, then she comes to counseling to rail about the injustice piled upon her. Tess depends on serial lovers. "I need to be in love!" she says in a way that demands that I do something about it.

While I agree that falling in love is one of the most ecstatic emotional highs a person can encounter, and while I myself adore being in love, I don't agree that falling in love necessarily leads to forever. Do you?

Being in love is a glimpse of heaven, for sure, but it's not the only way to enter.

There are many doors to ecstasy. That's what my seventy-nine-year-old friend Maggie inspires. "I've been in love two dozen times or more, and in between I've been frantic," she says

Being in love is a glimpse of heaven, for sure, but it's not the only way to enter.

with a twinkle in her eye, "but not since I turned seventy. Now," she says, "I'm in love, but I have no lover." Maggie's white hair is tucked up with clips, and some strands fall around her face. She hasn't made love for seventeen years. "There are many ways to love," she told me. "Many objects for my affection." I watched her closely. She wasn't in love, and she didn't have a lover. She was simply full of love, overflowing with love. You could tell it by the easy way she moved.

Maggie spends days in solitude, painting and practicing tai chi under the gazebo in the park. "When I'm sleeping in my hammock beneath the stars, the wonder of the universe merges with the wonder of my life. Lasting bliss comes to the spiritually ready, and you're not ready for that high, until your heart's been shattered."

We see two different women in two different stages—Tess in the first half of her life, Maggie in the second half of hers. Each stage—and woman—has its own beauty, meaning, and purpose. You really can't compare them. In the first half, the sexual urgings are the most compelling. That's when falling in love, sexual passion, and mating dominate. In the second half, desires stir in the distance while fresh urgings move forward.

The blessings of creativity and spirituality are calling. Somewhere in the midst of passing from youthful trembling to mature celebration, you start defining yourself as separate from emotional entanglements.

How many times have you said to yourself, "If I only would have known then what I know now?" Well, of course, when you're young, you can't know what you'll know when you're older. You can learn from others; however, you absolutely must flavor that borrowed knowledge with your own experience. Otherwise you remain permanently shallow. Walk your path, and allow the wise elders—who've been in and out of love countless times—to point you toward the everlasting.

Let Maggie's discovery that you can be in ecstasy without a lover bring you solace when you get down. Then, if ever your lover lets you down or when there's no lover in sight, you'll know where to turn for that oceanic rapture of being in love with life.

try this

1. Fall in love as much as you can. Fall in love with falling in love. Just don't make it the only thing you do.

2. Enjoy your broken heart. After all, that's part of being in love too, isn't it?

3. Okay, be dramatic. Suffer. Lean into the pain, don't shrink or hold back.

4. Read and write love poems. Ask the librarian to recommend a romantic poet.

5. If you're in the first half of your life, then consider the wisdom of the single elders who have probably been through what you're going through. If you're a single elder, pass on what you know to the young ones listening.

> Accustom yourself continually to make many acts of love, for they enkindle and melt the soul.
>
> —SAINT TERESA OF ÁVILA

Six Bedtime Routines

If you're tossing and turning and can't get to sleep, try one of these bedtime activities. Changing your nighttime habits is not only relaxing, it's fun.

1. Talk pillow talk. A soothing human voice will lull you to sleep faster than a blaring television. Listen to an audio book or make a pillow-talk pact with a telephone buddy. Swapping true-life stories, at a distance, safely tucked under your own sheets, is oh so relaxing.

2. Cuddle under the covers. Curl up with a teddy bear and a body pillow while listening to lullabies. It works for kids, and it will probably work for you too. At the very least, cuddling with a teddy bear will bring out your playful side, and that's healthy.

3. Eat early. Make plans to take yourself out for breakfast as soon as the sun comes up. Set the alarm so you don't sleep in.

4. Walk late. Get out of the house, and take a moonlight stroll. There is a new perspective under the stars. Carry a flashlight, a whistle, and maybe take along a big dog to boost your confidence.

5. Paint in the dark. Never force yourself to stay in bed just because it's after midnight. Get up and paint the walls, or express yourself on canvas. Tackling any creative project in the middle of the night will transform your self-image from plain to flamboyant.

6. Write what you know. Take your journal or your laptop to an all-night diner, and get your story down. Don't fret about good grammar or complete sentences. Save the editing for another sleepless night.

4

The *Best Revenge* Is a *Good Life*

A good life begins when you take charge. It begins when you step up to the plate, resolve that this is it, and whisper, "I can handle it." You can feel the power. In an instant you shed the overly cautious armor, and instead of playing it safe, you're stretching. Anyone can complain that life isn't fair. We all know that, but to have a life worth living is a whole other matter. That takes spunk. So here's to the spirit, spunk, and enterprise that goes into creating a life that couples often envy. Here's to love, laughter, and knocking their socks off.

Getting Cozy with the Gaps

What makes single life grim is the same thing that makes it captivating. It's the choices you make when nothing's going on that define you.

Victoria didn't decide to remain single. It's just what happened. Life is like that—it surprises you. You can be in search for one thing and discover another. You can't change everything, but you can change some things. What Victoria could change, she told me, was how she handled the gaps. "I'm comfortable with gaps," she says.

Gaps are empty spaces. We've all felt them. Those tiny quiet spaces where nothing's going on—like the empty space between one thing or another. We're alone, then we're not, we're alone again and then we're not. Sometimes we share our days and nights, and other times we sleep and eat alone. As we move through life, it's constantly changing, but it's hard to realize when you're in a gap. Like the empty space between sleep and waking up—before even opening your eyes, when your body feels heavy and it takes effort to move. "In those moments I'd much rather be cuddling," says Hugh, "but it's also that paralyzing moment of annihilation when I'm most connected to myself."

Gaps are the most torturous when you don't have a plan. For months your schedule is full, with interesting projects, dinners, and phone calls. And then out of the blue—nothing. Friends are busy, work is slow, and you don't feel like tackling more projects. We've all faced empty spaces—perhaps you've even craved them—yet when they arrive, which they always do, they're so unexpected and jarring. It's in those gaps that we come face to face with our little fears and demons.

> Gaps are the most torturous when you don't have a plan. It's in those gaps that we come face to face with our little fears and demons.

How do you handle gaps? Victoria says, "I don't know how my life will play out, but I do know the kind of person I want to be." She pays attention to those tiny breaks and treats herself gently. She knows they're coming, so she's prepared. "I have a routine that fights off terror. I turn to myself and to my higher power. I meditate and walk. I cherish the quiet time. I spend a day on the couch, I read, I go the gym, and take a sauna. By the end of the day I feel a sense of accomplishment and peace."

When do you feel the most alone *and* connected to yourself? For Paula, the gap between opening her front door and walking into the quiet, motionless house is a barren span that sucks the breath right out of her. That's when she misses her husband, who was once glad that she'd come home. Yet it's in her quiet house that she finds her spiritual power.

There are many spaces in a day, a week, or a year when there's no one with whom we can share our most intimate thoughts and understandings. There are times when no matter how hard we try to reach out, no matter how much we extend ourselves, and no matter how many people there are who care, we are standing still and motionless in our own awareness. That's when we need to really be there for ourselves. That's the measure of our spiritual determination.

A single who faces his spiritual side often outdistances others. It's the spiritual communion that sustains him. It's in the silence of the gap that we are more likely to embrace the Divine, the force of the universe that unites us all. In silence, we're able to hear our own wee voice giving us direction and good advice. God comes closer in those quiet moments and reminds us that all is well. That sweet assurance is enough to keep us going.

try this

1. Use the gaps for soul-searching and spiritual development. Compile a list of twenty-five spiritual activities that you'd like to investigate.
2. Take a meditation or yoga class. Meditating through the gap works well.
3. Do spiritual practice every day—a three-minute prayer works wonders.

4. Feed your soul. Put inspiring quotes on your front door, on the refrigerator, and next to the telephone. Read them often.
5. Be kind to yourself. Yes, it's hard, but try it.

> Instead of seeing the rug being pulled from under us, we can learn to dance on a shifting carpet.
>
> —THOMAS CRUM

Sex—Wait Cheerfully, Pursue Patiently

They say that women lie about their weight and dress size and that men lie about how much money they make or how much weight they can lift in the gym. I have no scientific proof, but I think everyone lies about their sex lives. We lie about how great it is and how often we have it. According to research, most of us think that other people have better sex lives than we do. Apparently that's a very common assumption, so please allow me to set the record straight. Most people are not living in sexual paradise. Most people are living in sexual misery.

Most people are not living in sexual paradise. Most people are living in sexual misery.

The problem is that almost every person wants sex! It's natural. It's our biology; the desire for sex is woven in our genes. Yet the truth is that satisfying sex is not that easy to get. There may be instant oatmeal, but there's almost never instant sex.

The *Cosmo* magazine girls would have us all believing that finding someone to have sex with is simple. All you have to do is look good, know a few techniques, smile, and been seen at the right places. Just watch one episode of *Sex and the City,* and you'll feel like a sexual loser—like you're really missing out. They're having great sex, so what's wrong with me? You might even spend big bucks on a pair of high heels and walk around until your feet are swollen, but unlike the girls on television, the only guys who hit on you are the ones with bad breath. If you're a guy, the challenge is just as daunting. Some nights you can't even get a lady to talk to you. Since most of us want to have sex with someone we're attracted to or with whom we feel a connection, we often end up spending the night in bed, alone again and feeling crappy.

But sexual feelings are very persistent. If you don't face your sexual feelings, they'll torture you. If you try to forget about your sexual desires, you'll become stiff and awkward. You'll become uncreative. The bad news is that while you never know exactly where or when you'll find the sex that you're seeking, the good news is that you can do some preparation. Be prepared. That's the law of Boy Scouts and the universe—if you prepare, sooner or later, sex will arrive.

Let's start by getting honest. You feel left out. You like sex, and you're not having it. Don't pretend that you're at peace with this crummy situation. You don't want to have sex with just anyone. You want to have sex with someone you like and are attracted to, but it seems that the only people available are the ones you're not attracted to. Yes, that really sucks!

But let's be realistic too. Sex is complicated for everyone. Just because your buddy adores his wife, that doesn't mean that they're having sex every night. And just because your best friend has a steady, that doesn't mean he's always in the mood. So stop assuming that everyone else is having sex. Sex really is the joker in the deck. Just because you want it, that doesn't mean you'll get it. In fact, the more you want it, the more needy you are, the less likely you are to find it. Focusing intently on getting sex makes you grabby. It's a little like playing cards. You get your turn, but not because you're throwing a tantrum.

What's the solution? Well, it differs for everyone, but the key is to not become jaded. There's a lot of waiting around in life, and waiting for sex is part of it. You want it, but your partner is watching *Star Trek*. You want it, and she's talking to her girl-friend on the phone. He's out of town, she's sleepy, he has a work presentation in the morning, she wants to finish reading her novel. Yes, indeed there is lots of waiting around. Waiting for the right person, then waiting for the right person to be in the mood.

It seems that finding sex is tied closely to a relaxed attitude while you're waiting. The prescription is simple: Wait cheerfully, and pursue patiently. Wait with open heart, and proceed with a twinkle in your eye. Complain about the lack of sex, and be good-natured about it. Remember, finding sex doesn't depend on how white your teeth are or how tight your abs are. Sex is about energy. It's more about energy than anything else.

try this

1. Know what your body wants and let it be a free, screaming, moaning machine.

2. Respect your own judgment, and don't let yourself be conned. If you ever feel you don't want to, you don't want to.

3. The two most important words to use in sexual encounters are "Yes" and "No."

4. Keep your sense of humor. Flip through the pages of a how-to sex book at the bookstore. That will be enough to keep you laughing until your next rendezvous comes along.

5. Rejoice that you have sexual urgings. It's these tender yearnings that dispel your lethargy, electrify you with alertness, and bring you to life. Hallelujah!

A person who has a healthy interest in sex is not a serious person. A person like that may be lighthearted, loving, caring, tender, dedicated, good-natured, and playful. But not serious.

—WILLIAM ASHOKA ROSS

Single Parents, Blessed and Busy

If you have children, you're blessed. If you're a single parent, you're blessed *and* busy.

"Raising my son and daughter was easy. Taking care of myself, earning money, paying the mortgage, the electric bill, the phone bill, mopping the floor, mowing the yard, making the beds, cleaning the toilet, washing the clothes, going to the grocery store, cooking breakfast, lunch, and dinner, walking the dog, paying the vet bill, squeezing in a social life, putting a tricycle together, remembering to get the oil changed and tires checked was hard. Balancing my checkbook was impossible.

There was always enough money to get by, never any extra," thirty-six-year-old Jessica told me. That's why she decided to make other arrangements. "I wanted a better living situation for myself and my kids." Jessica placed an ad in a local newspaper: "Looking for single mom with kids to share housing, child-care, and moral support." She interviewed four women and found that she had a lot in common with Lynn, a mother of an eight-year-old boy. After several months of talking it over, the two families moved in together. "By combining incomes, we were able to get a much nicer house," says Lynn. Both agreed that having another parent around the house who was going through the same experience was a relief. "We sit up at night after the kids fall asleep and laugh and joke about the trials and tribulations we go through," says Jessica, "and I don't feel so alone."

If you've got kids, you might consider combining your resources with another family. That's what Carmel Sullivan, a single mom, did after her divorce. She'd been talking to other single moms and found that they were dealing with the same loneliness issues that she was. Some suffered atrocious living conditions. Carmel founded *www.co-abode.com* to help single mothers connect with each other, to share resources, and to go home at the end of the day knowing they don't have to raise their children alone.

Living with another single mom can improve your situation tremendously. It cuts expenses, baby-sitting, and chores in half. "It makes chores a lot easier when two people are pitching in," says Jessica. "We switch off. I do dinner, she does cleanup. The kids enjoy living together too, they've become like brother and sisters."

Two families living under the same roof can be an enriching experience. When Jan's sister-in-law divorced Jan's brother, the two women—whose kids were already friends—decided to move in together. They carpool, have meals together, and the kids entertain each other, which has been a bonus, since that gives the moms a little private time of their own. Having someone in the same situation helps. Both the kids and the moms have companionship. The house is never empty—although it may be noisy—and there is always something going on.

You can be a fabulous single parent, you can raise fabulous children, and there is more than one way to do it. Children benefit from living in a village, and you won't be so tired when you're sharing the load. You children's well-being depends much more on your parental support than it does on a particular family structure. When you open your hearts to another family, you double the resources, double the love, and double the fun.

> **Children benefit from living in a village. You can be a fabulous single parent, you can raise fabulous children, and there is more than one way to do it.**

try this

1. Are you tired, financially strapped, or tired of living alone? If your answer is yes, you might consider creating a village by combining your household with another.

2. Do research on sharing households by visiting *www.co-abode.com.*
3. Talk the idea over with your kids. Ask for their input each step along the way.
4. Smile and be upbeat. Give a yell: "Hip, hip, hurray for our family!"
5. If you do combine your households, make a banner for your village.

> You can sort of be married, you can sort of be divorced, you can sort of be living together, but you can't sort of have a baby.
>
> —DAVID SHIRE

Pull Each Other Up

Ed has full custody of his three sons. Money was always tight. But things were especially difficult the year his boys were ages eight, eleven, and twelve. It was December, and Ed was planning on buying the boys bikes for Christmas. He'd saved all year and looked around for the best deals. Of course, the boys had in mind specific dirt bikes, and those were the ones he intended to buy. November was a month full with financial catastrophes. The transmission in his truck went out, the water heater was leaking, his oldest broke his leg, and Ed's construction job was in the middle of an unusually bad winter slump. Boys have big appetites, and Ed could barely keep food on the table, let alone buy a transmission, pay an emergency room bill, and buy a new hot-water tank. I'm sure you can put yourself in Ed's shoes and understand how discouraged and stressed he felt when he confided in his buddy Scott that he wouldn't be able to buy the bikes for Christmas.

Scott got busy and collected donations for bikes and groceries. At first Ed refused to take the money. He was embarrassed and felt like a failure, because "A man isn't a man if he can't take care of his family." Scott quickly set him straight: "Be a man, and allow us the pleasure of giving."

Ed was blessed by the gift. He was fortunate to have people around him who not only care, but in times of need take action. Not all single parents are as fortunate. When money is tight, keeping yourself together is difficult. But when you have kids and financial pressures, it's doubly hard. Many single parents don't have anyone to turn to, but I think that could change if all single parents paid more attention, noticed each other, and talked honestly about their situations. Shame, like the kind Ed felt, sometimes keeps single parents embarrassed and hiding.

Child-care costs, housing costs, health care, low-paying jobs, and no work are big hurdles for single parents. Betty, who works a low-wage job, has trouble affording school-related activities for her children. She's never been able to have a family holiday, and her kids don't have well-fitting, warm winter clothes. She has a hard time making ends meet, and she skips meals to get by. She has no time, no energy, no extra money for herself or for socializing. Despite the seemingly insurmountable challenges, she's resourceful. She places the emphasis on family loyalty and sees to it that kids are getting educated.

We all know that children thrive in stable families. The more nurturing children receive at home, and the safer they feel, the more likely they are to do well in school, form healthy relationships, and create better lives for themselves. We need policies that give low-income families the tools to create steady family lives. That's the smartest investment we can make. Single-parent households need predictable incomes, savings, and assets that can help them survive crises. They need good support systems. So let's all get busy.

Single-parent households need predictable incomes, savings, and assets that can help them survive crises. They need good support systems. So let's all get busy.

Single parents can help each other out, pull each other up, band together, draw close, and become a force for economic and political change. Schmoozing is fun, socializing is healthy, and making a difference in each other's lives and those of our children is the right thing to do. Our common humanity matters most. If we don't take care of each other and our children, who will? Problems that seemed unbearable are less daunting when we help each other out. How we as single parents behave toward other single parents has implications for every human being.

try this

1. Educate yourself and those around you about the issues facing single parents and children. Do you know how many single parents there are in your neighborhood? Do you know how many children are living in poverty in your city?

2. Pay attention. Is there a single-parent household that needs something you can provide? If you see a need, figure out a way to fill it.

3. Receive help. If you are in a bind, let someone know. It is not nice to only be on the giving end. It's a blessing to give, that's true, but if you're doing all the giving, you're depriving someone else of that pleasure.

4. Keep tabs on your elected officials, and make sure that they enact policies that support single parents.

5. Keep your chin up. A time will come when there will be time for you.

> There is a time to let things happen and a time to make things happen.
>
> —Hugh Prather

A Daughter, a Christmas Tree, a Pity Party

From the time Amanda was three years old, she liked Christmas trees and lights. I did too. And I liked those scenes of families dressed in red velvet, sipping eggnog, and singing carols as they hung carefully collected ornaments on perfectly shaped branches. I was never able to achieve that look. Choosing a Christmas tree was fun. However, putting it into my Volkswagen convertible, driving it home, positioning it in a stand, carrying it into the house, forcing it to stand up straight, decorating it, picking it up when it fell over, taking it down, putting away the decorations, and vacuuming up the needles was not fun.

Amanda's attention span for decorating was short. When she was a toddler, she'd rather play with the ornaments than hang them on the tree. As a youngster, she'd rather run next door to check out the Hansen's tree. When she was a teenager, she'd rather talk on the phone. I'm still ashamed to admit it, but every time I've decorated a tree, I've been cranky. In spite of my positive incantations—"You're having fun, you're making memories"—I wasn't able to convince myself, and my longed-for festive spirit turned into a pity party for one.

My intention was to eliminate all self-defeating thoughts, but no matter how hard I'd try to force them away, by December they'd seep back. In my crazy holiday state of mind, the reason that tree wouldn't stand up straight was because I didn't have a nice husband like my girlfriends did. Each December I was convinced that if I were tall, skinny, and blonde, I too would have a helpful, cheerful husband stringing the lights and straightening the tree.

Each December I was convinced that if I were tall, skinny, and blonde, I too would have a helpful, cheerful husband stringing the lights and straightening the tree.

And so it went. Amanda and I would pick out a tree, often more expensive than I could afford. I'd struggle to get it into the stand, bring it into the house, and decorate it by myself. I did it year after year. I was a slow learner. My behavior was ridiculous, and my negative attitude was getting us down. I warned myself often: Do something different and be quick about it.

Single parents have to be creative, and I'd risen to the task on many occasions. Instead of buying the $100 papier-mâché bowl that I coveted, I made one. When I wanted a kitchen table, I bought a lopsided one at a thrift store and fixed the leg. I've sewn a jacket and a bathrobe from a chenille bedspread that I bought for $5 at a garage sale. I'd negotiated a one-price deal at a swap meet on a boxful of Barbie dolls, a scooter, a plastic swimming pool, and a footstool. When I took the kids to the movies, I'd make popcorn at home and sneak it in in brown paper bags. My sack lunches were so appealing that Amanda's schoolmates envied her not having to eat in the cafeteria.

But when it came to a Christmas tree, I was stuck in the rut of believing there was only one way to do it. I was stuck believing that if I strayed from magazine images, my kid would feel deprived. She'd already come home crying because a couple of kids had teased her about being poor. "Honey, why do you think we're poor?" I asked. "We don't have a Nintendo," she said. "And we don't have cable, or an ice machine, or a VCR, or an SUV." It was true we don't have slick, shiny gadgets or drive a sleek car, but we did have love. "Some families are rich with things," I told her, "but you and I are rich with love." "We'll then, I'm deprived," she answered. And I agreed—she was appliance deprived.

I must have felt slightly guilty about depriving my darling of appliances, because I couldn't shake feeling like a Scrooge unless that tree was up. I didn't want my child to suffer in any way, no single parent does. I didn't want her to go without. And so I tried to purge my guilt by putting up a Christmas tree that I didn't want. Perhaps it symbolized all of our deprivations. Perhaps it was my feeble attempt to make amends for depriving her not only of appliances, but also of depriving her of a father, of brothers and sisters, and of all the imagined deprivations to come.

My atonement was ineffective. It never really works to do something you really don't want to do. Every time I put up a tree because I felt guilty, I grew more resentful. And that resentment was spoiling what joy we might have found. I desperately needed a poetic approach to Christmas.

On my morning walk around the block, I was delivered from my torment. Lying in the neighbor's yard was a large branch that had broken off in a windstorm. "Can I have that twig?" I asked. Visions of sugarplums danced in my head as I dragged that "twig" three blocks home, painted it white, stuck it in a pot of pebbles, and hung twinkle lights and silver stars from its branches. "It's our Charlie Brown tree," I told Amanda. When her friends asked, "What's that?" she'd tell them, "It's our Charlie Brown Christmas tree." We had that tree for several years. Whenever we went shopping, I'd proudly point out that Nordstrom's was decorating the aisle with twigs that looked exactly like ours.

After a couple of years with the white twig, I yearned for the smell of fresh pine, and we got a green tree again. The next year we even went to a tree farm and chopped one down. But it was different that time. The pressure was gone, and I was free. Since that white twig, we've had a couple of Noble firs, and even a flocked one. Then, a few years later at an art fair, I bought a five-foot wooden Santa that had been hand-painted by a local artist. We decorated him with tiny white lights and put our gifts around him. It was so joyful. We put on the music and drank sparkling cider. It took ten minutes total. We like him so much that now he stays in our living room through January. When we're finished with him, I simply unplug the lights and store him in a closet until next year.

Holidays can be a real downer for single parents, especially if guilt is plaguing your actions. Years from now the kids won't remember the shape or size of the tree. They won't remember how many gifts they got, but what they will remember is how it felt to be together. Put your emphasis on taking it easy, drinking eggnog, and having fun.

try this

1. Give a pity party for one, but don't ever let it last for more than one week at the max. Commiserate with a friend, but never with the kids. Tell your children that your being upset has nothing to do with them.

2. Do something different. You don't have to celebrate the holidays the same way every year. Just because you had a Christmas tree last year doesn't mean you have to have one this year.

3. Lavish kids with your good nature. Deprive them of appliances.

4. Use a poetic approach to holidays, and make the most of what you've got. Place the emphasis on eating cookies, not decorating.

5. Content yourself with simple gifts.

> The happier I have allowed myself to be, the happier my children have become.
>
> —WILLIAM MARTIN

Stand Up for Your Children

The first week of kindergarten, the teacher drew a graph on the blackboard and instructed all the students to come to the front and fill in one of the blank spaces with the number of people they had in their family. One by one each little kid walked to the board and wrote down a number—four, five, four, six, and so on.

Five-year-old Amanda—my daughter, an only child of a single mom—was embarrassed. "There's only mom and me in my family," she thought. "I wish I had a dad and brothers and sisters like all the other kids have." Amanda didn't want to do the assignment and hid in the back of the room behind the coat rack so that the teacher wouldn't notice. But the teacher did notice, and she called Amanda to the front of the room. "Go ahead, Amanda," the teacher insisted. "Write down how many people are in your family."

Amanda hated the assignment. She didn't understand why she had to do it. "After all, it was private information," she told me twenty years later. But Amanda obeyed and slowly wrote down "three." "I lied," she said. "I've always wished there were more people in my family."

That wasn't the end of the trouble over Amanda's single-parent household. In the fourth grade, a teacher said to Amanda, "I'm so surprised that you come from a single-parent family." "I thought it was a stupid comment," Amanda told me later, "and I wondered what she meant, but I didn't say anything about it." In a high school class on family life, another teacher read statistics about kids in single-parent families being more troubled as adults, but this time Amanda wasn't as shy about speaking out. "I thought the teacher was making generalizations about single parenting that he couldn't support." Amanda gave a report on a study that found that boys who grow up in mother-only families have better relationships with women later in life; daughters in such families are more likely to see their mothers as independent, strong women; both children have closer relationships with their parents. "There are both positives and negatives about being in a single-parent household, just like being in any family," Amanda said. "I thought the teacher should know the whole story."

As single parents, we need to be sensitive—without blowing things out of proportion—to the pressures of being a kid in a single-parent household. Every day, our kids face stereotypes and prejudices from teachers and classmates. That's a lot of pressure for a little person to bear. There are other burdens, too— burdens that the adults overlook.

As single parents, we need to be sensitive—without blowing things out of proportion—to the pressures of being a kid in a single-parent household.

Alex was seven and Peter was nine when their mom died. Dad worked long hours in a warehouse, and Alex and Peter learned to cook and clean right away. They took over most of the household chores. Alex did the cooking—muffin pizzas were his specialty. Peter did the cleaning—dirty dishes were his domain. They did the laundry, shopped for groceries, and cleaned the bathroom. Kids in single-parent households are often like that. They learn to take care of themselves early and to shoulder adult-sized duties. Frequently they worry about their parents. "My dad was so sad after Mom died that we didn't want to bother him," Peter said. "We did all the chores to help out."

Since kids have concerns that they don't mention, and since they might not have the skills to talk about what is troubling them, it's our obligation to understand from our child's perspective. Kids too have needs, hurts, longings, and disappointments. They go through difficult times just as you do. "No matter where I am, I'm always missing someone," ten-year-old Adam told me. "When I'm with Mom I miss Dad, when I'm with Dad I miss Mom."

Being a kid in a single-parent household has both advantages and disadvantages. It affects each kid differently depending on the circumstances. When they're going through a rough patch, they'll need you more than ever to be there for them. They'll need to feel safe and to know that no matter what, you'll always love them.

Now that she's an adult, Amanda says she only has a few minor complaints about being an only child of a single parent. Mostly they have to do with wanting someone else around to keep an eye on me so that I don't get into trouble.

try this

1. Tell your child through your words and your actions that it's perfectly normal to be from a single-parent household.
2. Don't speak badly about your child's other parent. The child's other parent is part of your child. Your child will wonder if you are thinking the same about him.

3. Put yourself in your kid's shoes, and ask yourself, "If I were my child, how would I want to be treated?" Remember, it's a lot of responsibility to be a kid in a single-parent household.

4. Be a rabble-rouser for children. Find one little cause on behalf of children and speak out.

5. Buy a sparkling beverage, gather a group of single parents, and give a toast: "Here's to all of us who struggle every day to make our decisions based on what is right for our children. Here's to us!"

> If you bungle raising your children, I don't think whatever else you do well matters very much.
>
> —JACQUELINE KENNEDY ONASSIS

Small Victories Add Up

When you fall off a horse it's best to get back on, and that's exactly what Alice and eight-year-old Charlie did. The divorce from Charlie's father would be final on Friday. On Saturday, Dad was getting married again, and the following week he was moving 800 miles away. Dad asked Charlie to attend the wedding, but Charlie adamantly refused. "The news of his remarriage and moving is so shocking," Alice said, "that I feel like I fell off a horse." She repeated it four or five times during our session, and as Alice talked, Charlie drew pictures of houses on fire and of horses. "Charlie," I asked, "is there anything you'd like to do on Saturday?" "Go horseback riding," he answered.

Alice and Charlie had never been horseback riding. "Honey, if you'd like to go to the wedding, it's okay with me. Your father loves you very much." "Nope," Charlie insisted, "I want to go horseback riding!" He said it firmly enough to convince Alice to call a dude ranch in Wyoming and take Charlie on a vacation. They had a spectacular time. Big heartaches, small victories, they add up.

> **Big heartaches, small victories, they add up. That's the way it is.**

That's the way it is. Even when you're devastated, the smallest gesture from a stranger can get you through. When you're least expecting it, life gives you signs that help you know you'll make it. "I broke my leg and was in a cast," James said, "and a teenager held my car door open while I put my groceries away." "A librarian patiently waited as I searched my purse and diaper bag for the overdue book," Ann said. "Her patience was the boost I needed when I was so frazzled. Then, when my baby sitter quit, a neighbor directed me to a friend of a friend who had a relative from Mexico staying to attend college. Eighteen-year-old Maria became our baby sitter and surrogate big sister for two years. She read and sang to us in Spanish, she made us sugar doughnuts."

Really worthwhile things slip in slowly. They happen gradually, they add up, they multiply. Joseph broke up with his fiancée three months before the wedding. "It was the hardest thing I've ever done, but I knew it was right." He didn't know anyone when he took a job at Yellowstone National Park waiting tables. For months he was lonely. One afternoon he waited on a woman traveling through, and one thing led to another. The woman offered Joseph a job in her restaurant in San Francisco and Joseph took it. He worked round the clock learning the business. The two formed a partnership and opened a second restaurant. Joseph had dinner with his ex-fiancée and in the six years since they parted she had victories too. She'd quit her job and had gone to graduate school. She bought a wooden boat, refinished it, and became an expert craftswoman.

Most of us don't win the lottery or become "discovered" overnight. Instead, our lives unfold gradually, and those delicate moments set our path in another direction without our even noticing.

> **Most of us don't win the lottery or become "discovered" overnight. Instead, our lives unfold gradually, and those delicate moments set our path in another direction without our even noticing.**

We have so much to go through in order to become ourselves. You've probably had times when you thought you'd "arrived," when all of your hard work had paid off, when all was right with your world. But there is always more to go through, more to discover, more pleasures, more pain, and more lessons. Life is not static. It's ever-changing, and we're all growing. Single life is brimming with small and steady victories. Love, whatever its form, surrounds us. When someone asks you, "How's your love life?" take the victorious road and answer, "Love surrounds me, life is full."

try this

1. Look back for a moment. Isn't it amazing how far you've come? Give yourself credit; you earned it.

2. Keep the faith! Expect a positive outcome even if the signs point in another direction.

3. Remember that unexpected acts of kindness are messages from the Divine assuring you that everything is okay.

4. When someone asks you, "How's it going?" answer, "Good things are coming."

5. When someone asks you, "How's your love life?" answer, "Love surrounds me, life is full."

> If you help others you will be helped, perhaps tomorrow, perhaps in one hundred years, but you will be helped.
>
> —GURDJIEFF

Marriage Envy

Helene and Julie go way back. Helene is single; Julie is married. They met the first day of college, and from that first meeting they were intrigued with one another. Julie, from San Francisco, was sophisticated in that city sort of way. Helene, a free spirit from Montana, liked open spaces and country music. Her laughter was contagious.

From the beginning they hung out with each other. Julie taught Helene to drink wine and eat artichokes, and in exchange Helene taught Julie to ride horseback and go hiking. They majored in psychology, joined the same sorority, played bridge instead of studying, and danced to the Beatles. For four years they were buddies. They double-dated and married their college sweethearts.

After graduation they parted, and the Goddess of Destiny guided their lives. While Julie went straight for the American dream, Helene entered the school of hard knocks. Julie raised two sons and followed her executive husband across the country as he climbed the corporate ladder. She read cookbooks and cooked gourmet. She had it all—a part-time career and a beautiful family. She was a registered nurse, a wife, and a very proud mother. Helene wanted to travel the direct route to happiness, too, but fate took her on the scenic loop. After eleven years of marriage, her husband Mark was killed in a car accident, and she was left a young widow and a single mom. She pushed through grief, rearranged her goals, and tackled single parenting. She worked as a hostess and then as a waitress. When her kids started school, Helene went back part-time, too. Eventually she got a degree from the culinary institute, opened a bistro, and wrote a cookbook. Over the years, Julie and Helene kept in touch with a twice-yearly letter or card.

After years of being apart, the goddess watching over must have interceded because Julie and Peter moved from Cincinnati to Seattle, where Helene lives, and bought a house just two minutes away. Now the two college friends were neighbors. Once settled in her new home, Julie invited Helene to dinner. Peter, attentively by Julie's side, poured drinks and assisted in the kitchen. The three of them reminisced about their college days, when Peter and Mark, Helene's husband, were soccer stars. Peter cleaned up the kitchen as Helene and Julie looked through piles of old photographs.

"On the outside, the evening was fabulous," Helene told me. "I was glad to be with old friends again, but on the inside

I was trembling. It was all too surreal for me to relax. I wanted to scream, 'My God, Julie lives the married life that I dream of for myself!'"

Marriage envy slowly seeped into Helene's heart that night. It wasn't that Helene hated her life. It wasn't that her life was awful, it was just that a little corner of her heart longed for a handsome, doting husband—a husband who took care of her, the way Peter took care of Julie. Helene drove home and fell into a slump.

Helene didn't confess her condition until months later. The two friends were sitting at an outdoor cafe, sipping chai soy lattes and sharing a gigantic cinnamon roll when a twinge of "She has it all" came over Helene. Right in the middle of Julie saying, "We're going to our beach house for a week," a hot flash of comparison grabbed Helene's attention. Comparison has no place in friendship, but Helene quickly got lost in ruminating. "Julie has a beach house and I'm a failure." It was a delusion that sometimes got the best of her.

"I wish I had a life like yours," Helene blurted out. Ignoring the surprised look on Julie's face, she went on. "Married life is easier." Helene didn't like feeling envious, and admitting that she felt that way was embarrassing, but for the sake of their friendship, she made a feeble attempt at confessing it. If she didn't, she thought their friendship might fall stagnant or, even worse, they'd grow apart. That she couldn't bear.

"I'm so sorry that you've had such a struggle," Julie said. "You didn't deserve it."

"I envy you and I feel like such a failure," Helene said out loud.

"Do you know that I sometimes envy you and your single life?" Julie sighed.

That got Helene's attention. "What could you possibly envy about my life?" she asked.

"I envy your spirit, your freedom, and all your experiences. You have such a wide variety of friends. Your life is so big," Julie answered.

That afternoon they walked around the Saturday Market. They bought bouquets of flowers, hazelnuts, snap peas, and sweet onions. "I envy that you can decorate your house exactly the way you want," Julie went on. "Being married, I compromise in every room."

They had a ball, giggling and listing their secret envies to each other. For each envy that Helene listed about married life, Julie had a matching one about single life. Helene envied Julie's financial security; Julie envied Helene's financial freedom. Helene envied companionship, while Julie envied independence. "I envy your strength and determination," Julie said. "I'm floundering to find my personal direction."

Helene left Julie's presence feeling lighter. She did have a full life. She'd survived. She made conscious choices. She'd expanded beyond her college dream and gone on to create a wide, open life. She was an independent woman of experience.

Marrieds and singles have a contribution to make to each other. In order to keep those friendships thriving, you have to nurture them, just like you'd nurture any relationship. You have to be honest and flexible. You have to gain understanding of the other perspective. No matter how well adjusted and content you are as a single, you will sometimes feel like a third wheel around happily married couples. Some singles complain that they were dropped by marrieds, while other singles let their married friends drift away.

It's not easy to admit, but we've all been envious. Regardless of our marital status or how content we feel, envy can pop up when we least expect it. Your friend shares a tidbit about the pleasures of married life, and suddenly you're wishing you were married. That's a crucial moment. You can either slink away, or say nothing. Or you can say something like, "I'm happy for you, and if I were married I'd like that too." You might say, "Please be patient with me, I'm going through a bout of marriage envy." It's usually best to address what's going on. Saying it out loud helps the ache pass more quickly. That's what brings us closer. It's when we keep our struggles to ourselves that the distance between us and our married friends grows wider.

> **It's not easy to admit, but we've all been envious.**

try this

1. Keep your options open—don't exclude marrieds from your social circle. Marrieds can benefit from singles and vice versa.

2. Whenever you come down with a case of marriage envy, admit it out loud. Ask your closest married friend if he or she might be willing to play a round of the "What I envy about you is . . ." game. That will give you a larger perspective.

3. Put yourself in your married friend's shoes and you'll see that they have plenty of challenges, too.

4. Avoid the comparison trap. When you compare yourself to someone else, you'll either end up feeling smug or you'll end up feeling lousy. There are no winners in the comparison game—someone always has it better than you, and someone always has it worse.

5. Which married friend has been a blessing in your life? Drop him or her a card and tell them so.

> Friendship is the only relationship that you have because you really want it, there's nothing keeping you together other than that you want to be.
>
> —JEAN THEISEN

Enormous Dating Hurdles

I had my first date as a single parent when my daughter, Amanda, was four years old. I hadn't realized how much she didn't want to share me until he came to pick me up. Amanda answered the door, kicked him in the shins as hard as she could, and said, "Leave my mother alone." Fortunately my date was very good-natured and admired her spunk. Even though I was mortified, he remained positive, appreciating her directness and spirit.

Peter started dating again when his sons were eight and twelve. They didn't like it one bit, and they showed it by refusing to make conversation. They'd answer the dates' questions with shrugs or one-word responses and then leave the room. Often they'd vie for Peter's attention by loudly fighting with each other. When Peter would ask the kids if they liked the woman he was dating, they'd say, "She's got a mustache," or "She's got nose hairs," or "She stinks," or "She looks like a frog."

The process of dating when you have children is not a walk in the park. Your children don't want to share you—it's as simple as that. Many kids of single parents never get over wishing that their parents would get back together, so they aren't going to make it easy for you to see someone else. There are exceptions however. Sometimes it's the adults who make it difficult for the child.

Billy was five years old when Anna began dating Tony. From the beginning Billy took a liking to Tony and his truck, and Tony responded by paying attention to Billy. Every time he came to see Anna, he'd bring a little present for Billy or make a special effort to include him. It was a love affair for the three of them for several years. But then Anna and Tony broke up, and Billy was left in the middle. He was stuck with having to cope with another loss and prepare for another stand-in Dad. Anna paraded lots of men through Billy's life. Some were nice, and some were downright mean, he says. Now that Billy is eighteen, he thinks it would have been better if his mom hadn't dated so many guys.

Some kids are just plain smarter than the parents. They see through things very quickly. Sixteen-year-old Abbey hates her mother's choice in boyfriends—for good reason. She chooses losers who either drink too much, can't keep a job, or lie. "My mom thinks she needs a man around," Abbey told me in counseling, "but she doesn't. I wish she'd see that she could do better."

Your children are affected by all your dating decisions. If you're bringing your dates into the house when your children are around, know that they see more than you think they do. They know what's going on. The people you choose to hang out with will have an impact on your child's life. If you're having ups and downs while dating, your children will pick up the vibes. If you're upset, your kids will be upset too. What bothers you will bother them. There's a lot of dating fallout, and children sometimes get it double if both parents are single and dating.

As a single parent, you have enormous hurdles. It's hard to meet your needs and your child's needs. It's hard to juggle everything, and it's even more challenging to figure out when to involve another person. Perhaps you'll have to forgo dating until the kids are out of the house, but maybe by then you'll be smarter and they'll be more tolerant. Perhaps by then they'll be so involved in their own dates that they won't be supervising yours.

try this

1. Make a pledge to put your children's needs above your dating needs.
2. Tell your kids that they are number one in your life. If you're dating, make it clear by your words and your actions that you love them best.
3. Show affection to your date in private.
4. Protect your kids from the ups and downs of your love life. It's best to keep your dating life separate until you're absolutely sure that your children will benefit from knowing another adult.
5. When you blow it with your children, which you sometimes will, apologize, learn the lesson, and do it differently next time.

Misery is when grown-ups don't realize how miserable kids can feel.

—SUZANNE HELLER

A Houseful of Housemates

When you're single, connections with others are broader and they grow wider. It's not just one person that you're involved with but many, and they fulfill different needs.

Four housemates—Greg, Henry, Elle, and Bette—live in a big old house on a tree-lined street in a neighborhood of big old houses. Henry and Elle bought the house together six years ago, and Greg and Bette moved in a year later when the renovations were completed. They all like living together and have no plans to move. A 1952 vintage poster for a movie entitled *We're Not Married,* starring Ginger Rogers, Fred Allen, and Marilyn Monroe, hangs in the front entry. In the romantic comedy, five couples find out that they're not legally married and are rather overjoyed about it. The movie has its twists and turns. In the end the sanctity of marriage survives, but it gets good-natured ribbing in the process. The four housemates, not wanting to be mistaken for couples, pasted their individual head shots over the actors' faces so that when visitors drop by they know instantly that the four housemates are single.

It's a communal household, with a percentage of ownership designated for each member. They share expenses and upkeep based on a legal contract. It works well and gives them the benefit of owning a home without the entire financial burden.

They enjoy the playful, affectionate camaraderie and especially the coed balance. Henry and Bette had a sexual relationship for a brief time, but not anymore and it's no longer an issue. Elle is the only one in a committed relationship. The others date, but no one is actively looking for a permanent partner. Two are "married to their careers" and Greg is "married" to medical school. Henry is the father of an eleven-year-old son who spends every other weekend and holidays at the "Not Married House."

When I asked them if they liked being single, I could tell that they were familiar with this line of questioning because they answered in unison, "What's wrong with being single?' And then again they answered in unison, "Nothing, absolutely nothing."

In a society that seems defined by relationships, there are lots of assumptions about singles. Contrary to popular opinion, not everyone wants to get married.

In a society that seems defined by relationships, there are lots of assumptions about singles. The main one is that singles are unhappy and desperately searching for a partner. People have options, so they marry later. They get out of marriages that aren't fulfilling. People live longer and have a variety of relationships. Just because a person exercises some untraditional options doesn't mean that their relationships are shallow.

All relationships—housemates, lovers, friends—have a higher purpose, a meaning that goes beyond what it might seem to be in the beginning. Housemates at first glance might seem only to be sharing a space, but what they share is more than a living arrangement. Just as when friends hang out together, their connection is more than a social outing. It's a coming together of spirits who participate in each other's lives. We learn about ourselves from each other. It's a beautiful process of shaping and shining us into the best versions of ourselves.

Like an orchestra, when you pool your talents, there's harmony in working together. When you laugh, talk, and joke with a friend or a housemate, you get more done and are energized. Love infuses itself into our friendships. That's the nature of love, and once a person has a place in your heart, they have a place forever. It really doesn't matter whether you're housemates, tennis partners, or golfing buddies. What matters is that you've come together and are enriched, refined, and improved.

Now the cat is out of the bag. The goose is out of the bottle. The truth is known. You can't participate in the fiction that there's only one way to have meaningful connections. You can find surprise with a houseful of housemates or comfort confiding in a friend. You can laugh and relax with sidekicks, or you can smile and ask how a colleague's day is going.

When you hold these sweet souls in the light, when you appreciate and honor the steadfast contributions they're making, you unlock the door to special times and understanding.

try this

1. When looking for housemates, consider carefully what qualities you are looking for. Living together goes beyond the convenience of sharing space.

2. Before you become a housemate, talk over all the details and your expectations. It's better to talk over house rules first to avoid unnecessary misunderstandings later.

3. When someone asks you, "Why isn't a cute person like you married?" answer them with "What's wrong with a cute person being single?" Say it with a smile and twinkle in your eye, and they'll wonder what makes you so cheery.

4. Follow through on your generous impulses toward others. If a friend, housemate, neighbor, colleague, or other human being needs you, don't hesitate to stand by them.

5. Give a toast to housemates and human kindness! Here's to the sweet spirit of generosity, to the soul of understanding, to the heart of sharing. Here's to housemates, friends, and buddies.

Do not protect yourself by a fence, but rather by your friends.

—CZECH PROVERB

My Declaration of Independence

No more sitting around
waiting for someone to call.
It's Saturday, and I'm stepping out.
I've got three fun things to do.
And I'm just the person to do them.
Join me if you can.
I'm not waiting.
I'm here! It's me!
I light up the room.

5

No One
Can Love

You More
Than You

Can Love
Yourself

Each day presents us with an opportunity to become more compassionate. Isn't that grand? We're learning to care for ourselves. Compassion is empathy for our struggles and blunders. It's forgiving our mistakes and admitting our shortcomings. It's knowing that even though we've messed up and made a fool of ourselves, we're willing to give ourselves another chance. Compassion is the gentle forgiveness of our own foibles. When we love and accept who we are, we are not afraid to grow, to learn, or to change. We're glad to be alive, and it shows.

A Leap Worth Taking

People often ask me, "Why? Why? Why?" As in, "Why is this happening to me?" or "Why am I still single?" and "Why can't I meet someone?" They don't like being in the single segment. They're miserably lonely. They feel awful. They're uneasy, irritable, depressed, and edgy. They hurt. They're impatient. They want a relationship to take the pain away, and as a result they grab for one—one right after the other. Or they withdraw, close down, and become immobile.

Singleness is not a catastrophe. It's not a tragedy, a calamity, or an affliction. It's an honorable platform. It pushes us to grow up even when we don't want to. Even when we're wallowing, moaning, or complaining, singleness shakes and shoves us into taking the leap from wanting someone to being someone.

Singleness is not a catastrophe. It's not a tragedy, a calamity, or an affliction.

When singles ask "Why?" I know it's because they're feeling bad about their own situation. At the bottom of the question is a bag of self-doubt. They think perhaps that they're not thin enough, strong enough, rich enough, smart enough, pretty enough. They're beating themselves up with self-incrimination. From their perspective, the whole world is populated with hand-holding couples, and as singles they feel so left out. They want to be in love too.

Falling in love has nothing to do with being thin or rich or deserving. Being in love has nothing to do with whether or not we are good. It's not the Academy Award for best performance. Falling in love has nothing to do with whether we deserve it or not—

Being single has nothing to do with being a good person or a bad person.

and neither does being single and not in love. Being single has nothing to do with being a good person or a bad person. It has nothing to do with our looks, our weight, or our pocketbook. Singleness is not a measuring stick.

That's the leap we're being called to take. The leap from thinking we're not okay to knowing that we are. The leap from "I can't do this, it's too hard" to "This is hard and I'm doing it." The leap from "I want a special love" to "I *am* a special love." The leap from "God is out to get me" to "This is the way it is right now."

The leap from "God is punishing me" to "God is helping me," and to go from "God is out to get me" to "God is working with me," are the biggest leaps of all. Leaping from happily married to happily single is like swinging on a rope to cross a canyon. Nothing left to do but leap and keep praying. And I'm still praying.

It's a leap of faith to face the full reality of our single situation and being able to take it all in. We leap like that when we live with the precariousness of being single, the heartache, the uncertainty, and the loneliness, and we take the leap from doubting that love is coming to trusting with all our heart and soul that it is. Doubting that love is coming makes us uneasy and nervous. Knowing that love is coming fills us with joy and gladness. That is a leap worth taking.

try this

1. Take the leap from "I doubt that love is coming" to "I know love is coming."
2. Take the leap from "I want somebody to love" to "I *am* somebody to love."
3. Take the leap from "I can't do this" to "I am doing this."
4. Take the leap from "God is punishing me" to "God is working with me."
5. Take the leap and keep on praying, "Dear God, help me to accept love as it is given even though it may not come in the package I requested."

I have learned not to worry about love, but to honor its coming with all my heart.

—ALICE WALKER

Think Outside Your Pattern

Sometimes singles complain that they keep attracting the wrong man, the wrong woman, the wrong relationship. What they really mean is that they are attracted to the wrong man, wrong woman, wrong relationship. They're stuck in an unconscious pattern that may reflect unmet childhood needs. They're holding on to emotional pain. They lack the self-esteem to put a stop to hurting themselves; they lack the confidence to step out of pain and step up to being fabulous.

For example, Elizabeth has been thinking about her past relationships. She's had an epiphany about her patterns and what she wants in a partner.

The last two guys were Phil and Frank. Phil was available, warm, and there for her. He called when he said he would, kept his word, and was sensitive to her needs. He was kind, considerate, and loving. He wanted the best for her and encouraged her to follow her dreams. The other guy was Frank. You guessed it. He and Phil were as opposite as opposites could be. Frank was available when he wanted to be. He called when wanted to, and that usually didn't coincide with when he said he would. He could be considerate on occasion, but he wasn't consistent. Elizabeth never knew what to expect—they could be close one evening, then Frank would be distant and cold the next.

Elizabeth liked Phil, but she was hooked on Frank. And so the relationships went like this. Frank got close and moved away. Phil got close, and Elizabeth moved away. That's the way it was until fate and circumstances intervened and they all parted.

Once Elizabeth started thinking about it, a little light bulb turned on. She's been wrapped up in the angst of grasping and longing for a man who really isn't there. Growing up, her father was emotionally distant in the same way Frank was distant. Until she saw the correlation, she was hooked on that push and pull. But once she saw the pattern, she was ready and able to move on.

What a fabulous revelation! What a tremendous opportunity. To be single and come to an understanding about relationship patterns and unconscious needs. What a wonderful opportunity to meet, date, and get to know as many different people as you can and get clear about what is important to you. Elizabeth says that she wants a "Phil." Not Phil personally, but rather what Phil represents. In fact, "I want a Phil" is her metaphor, one that really means she's ready to be close to someone who is ready to be close to her.

If you think that you might be stuck in a pattern of "I'm not good enough," or "Something's wrong with me," try to look at it from a different angle. You're so lucky to be single. You have time to get rewired. You can work on your self-defeating patterns and change the beliefs that no longer serve you. Even a broken heart can be a blessing—we're all more teachable when we're vulnerable and in pain. Being single gives us a perspective that we can't have when we're swooning, holding on, worrying about, chasing, or taking care of a partner.

> Even a broken heart can be a blessing—we're all more teachable when we're vulnerable and in pain.

Honor your own feelings, needs, desires, and thoughts. If we don't honor ourselves, we will not be honored by others. Recognize your patterns so that you can respond appropriately instead of automatically. Turn away from things that hold you back so that you can go forward. Think about your relationships, and say goodbye to those that pull you down and hello to those that pull you up.

try this

1. Do a personal inventory. Have you ever repressed your personality, desires, beliefs, or limited your freedom in order to stay in a relationship? If the answer is yes, that means you were dependent and fearful.

2. Do this homework: Write two pages about your relationship with your parents. Write two pages more about your adult romantic relationships. Write two pages more about patterns that are self-defeating.

3. Give yourself a motto to live by.

4. Recruit three friends to help you rewire. Ask them to write letters of testimony about you. Ask them to include what they like about you, what qualities they see in you, and any suggestions they have. Ask them to mail the letter to you. Keep those letters in a special spot, and read them over again and again while you're rewiring your patterns.

5. Start your day by saying out loud, "I'm a fabulous catch." Say it three times. Don't merely think it. Say it out loud, and it will stick with you longer.

Some of the clearest thinking we do about relationships occurs while we're not in one.

—MARIANNE WILLIAMSON

Attractive Has Very Little to Do with Looks

Jack looked at my feet one day and said, "Honey, you've got pretty feet!" Stunned, I looked at my feet and asked, "I do?" "Yes," he said, "You really do." At first I couldn't believe it. I'd never paid any attention to my feet before. I hardly knew I had them, but after he said that, I started noticing my feet. I thought to myself. "If he thinks they're pretty, I'd better take care of them."

Ten years after his death, I was trying on shoes at Nordstrom's in Seattle. The handsome clerk helping me said, "You've got pretty feet." "I take care of them," I proudly announced. "Well, it sure shows," he said. "You should see what I see! Most people don't care at all about their feet. I've seen terrible feet, but yours are nice."

A couple of years later I was invited to a Japanese-style dinner party. I didn't know beforehand that I would have to take my shoes off at the door. Since there weren't enough slippers to go around, I had to go barefoot through the buffet line. As I was standing in line, the woman in front of me looked at my feet and said, "You've got pretty feet." "Yes, I know," I said, "I take care of them." She looked really shocked by my honesty. "I don't like my feet," she said. "They're ugly." What a pity, I thought to myself. Most people probably have no idea how beautiful feet can be.

Isn't it amazing that a loving compliment can change a life forever? Everyone has something beautiful about them. Some people have beautiful hair, some flawless skin, some sparkling eyes, some loving hearts. But not everyone knows it. Sometimes we're so busy comparing ourselves to others—like those slim models in

> **Isn't it amazing that a loving compliment can change a life forever?**

the magazines—that we don't recognize the beauty in ourselves. I'm sick of plastic looks and airbrushed beauty. That doesn't get us anywhere. But when a person says something honest, from one heart to another, that honesty has the power to change a life forever. That's what all the people who love us do, no matter how or where or when they pass out of our lives. They help us recognize our beauty and love ourselves in a way we never did before. My sweetheart telling me that I had pretty feet was such a small thing, but it had an impact on me. It stayed with me, and to this day, thirty-some years later, I look at my feet and think of him.

You're always connected through love to the people you love. Isn't it true? Think of the people who have loved you. Perhaps you're no longer in touch with the person who told you that they loved your radiant smile, the shine of your hair, the way your nose wrinkled, the sweetness of your voice. Yet you remember their words. All those things that made you beautiful then are still yours—even if the person is gone. Your beauty is untouchable. It's yours. You own it.

I'm not talking plastic beauty here, that is, the useless battle to look good, to flatten your tummy, have white-white teeth, to erase the lines. I'm talking about acknowledging our natural beauty, that God-given loveliness that makes us different from one another. I like my pretty feet. What do you like about yourself? Hands? Eyes? Ears?

Most people talk about having a partner as a source of great fulfillment, but we seldom mention the fulfillment that comes from appreciating our own beauty. And while having another person compliment our looks feels great, it's only a springboard for us to begin to appreciate our own exquisite bodies.

When it comes right down to it, being attractive has very little to do with looks. It has more to do with an inner glow that comes from appreciating our own beauty and taking good care of ourselves. It has to do with attracting, which is what a magnet does. That's a magnet's inherent power. Personal attractiveness is also a kind of power that comes when you can honestly acknowledge your loveliness.

try this

1. Don't be shy! What is beautiful about you?
2. Don't be ashamed to be attractive. Accept compliments graciously, and run with them.
3. Take care of your feet. Get a pedicure this week.
4. Remember your last lover? What did he or she find beautiful about you? You own that beauty. It's yours, even if your lover is gone.
5. Be generous with compliments. Receiving one can really give a single person a boost.

> Nothing makes a woman more beautiful than the belief that she is.
>
> —SOPHIA LOREN

Dance with Your Wild Side

Karen, a no-nonsense woman, gave herself a new name. Roxie. Roxie's a wild girl. Roxie's fun. Roxie is daring. She flirts, winks, and goes contra dancing. She sits next to strangers just because they look interesting. Roxie rode the third-class sleeper across India—Karen would never do that. Karen's new identity serves her very well. Whenever she gets nervous, worried, or feels like shrinking, she whispers to herself, "What would Roxie do in this situation?" Roxie always has a unique and colorful solution.

When you do the unexpected, life may not open up all at once. In fact, nothing major may happen at all. But the tiniest shift in demeanor can turn a dull moment into a memorable minute. The guy you snuggle up to at the bar won't be your soul mate, and you may never talk to the stranger on the bus again, but those conversations add spark to the day. It's working for Karen. When I told my client Paul about Roxie, he followed Karen's lead and christened himself Duke. The very next time I saw him he said, "Duke was really on fire last night!" Right after that, I decided to bring my artsy girl out of hiding—Artsy Lily's her name.

If you're going to have stories to talk about in your old age, you've got dance with your wild side while you can still move. You don't have to go skydiving or strike up conversations with every stranger you come across. You've got to loosen up and be uninhibited. You have to be slightly silly, a wee bit outrageous, and open to the unexpected. Your wild side doesn't have to be crude. Instead, your wild side can simply be unconstrained and free.

Still not getting it? Think about it this way. Have you ever overheard someone talking in a restaurant, and what he or she is saying touches you in such a way that you want to say hello to them, to this perfect stranger? You want to go to them and say, "Hey, I heard what you said and I think you're wonderful and I want you to know I'm with you." But you don't do it. You're afraid that the other person might say, "So you were eavesdropping?" or "Who's this creep?" Well, you can think about all the reasons you have for not talking to them, or you can do that unexpected thing, make that unexpected move, and take your chances.

When was the last time you did something totally opposite of what you would normally do? Remember how good it felt?

> **When was the last time you did something totally opposite of what you would normally do? Remember how good it felt?**

We make so many excuses to ourselves for not being spontaneous and free. I've noticed we have two kinds of excuses that we give ourselves: excuses for doing something, and excuses for *not* doing something. In my experience, the excuses we give ourselves for *not* doing something are the ones that eat us up the most. They just nag at us something terrible, don't they?

Yet what we really have a hard time forgiving ourselves for is missing the moment, missing out on spontaneity. Our lives are filled with "I should have done . . ." or "I should have said . . ." or "I wish I had . . ." We can't seem to forgive ourselves for not doing the unexpected. Or, to say it another way, we can't forgive ourselves for only doing what's expected.

So here's my challenge to you. Reacquaint yourself with your wild side, that undomesticated, untamed spirit lying dormant—that fanciful lady inside who is daring and unafraid. Introduce yourself to her. She's been squelched for such a long time. Bring her out of her box and give her a name.

try this

1. Devote one day to doing something so daring that even you can't believe that you're doing it.
2. Who is your inner "Roxie"? Give yourself a wild name, and think of yourself as that character.
3. Ask yourself, "What would my unchained, spirited self do?"
4. Imagine yourself fearless around the opposite sex. Make eye contact, and smile at three strangers per week.
5. Don't tell your mom.

You're only given a little spark of madness. You mustn't lose it.

—ROBIN WILLIAMS

Hold Hands and Give Chocolate

Catherine needs two things for a celebration—chocolate and hand-holding. They've become her trademarks. She prefers walking hand-in-hand with friends, and she gives chocolate for the simplest of reasons. When the man Allison was seeing stopped calling without an explanation, Catherine gave Allison four frog-shaped chocolates. That livened up what was a little disconcerting, and everyone liked them so much that Catherine gives frog-shaped chocolates once a year to all her unmarried friends. When Carl broke his leg, Catherine gave chocolate to cheer him up and get the healing started. When the cast came off, she took him for a hand-holding afternoon stroll.

> When you take note of a commonplace event in your friend's life, you refresh the connection between you.

When you take note of a commonplace event in your friend's life, you refresh the connection between you.

When you hold hands with someone dear, you're responding to the need we all have to be close and feel safe.

Families and friendships flourish when shored up with celebrations. We're not just talking about the big events like birthdays and holidays, but about the milestones—like getting a promotion at work, losing ten pounds, or buying a house. Acknowledging those happenings is the sparkle that enlivens an ordinary day and draws us close. Married couples have built-in celebrators in each other, so as a single you might have to do more planning and arranging. But regardless of whether the celebration is planned or spontaneous, it's absolutely essential to commemorate the passages. Even if you're the one who initiates your own event, celebrations are invigorating.

When Kristine graduated from high school, her mother threw a big party for family and friends to mark the milestone. When Kristine graduated from college, her parents and grandparents flew from out of state to attend. They celebrated at breakfast with smiles, reminiscing, and pats on the back. They celebrated at dinner with speeches and toasts. It was a happy occasion. Afterward the family flew home, and Kristine moved into an apartment with a roommate. She started a new job, worked very hard, and got a promotion. When Kristine got her raise, she decided to throw herself a party to celebrate just like her family had done for her in the past. She called her friends, served good food, and had a great time.

Get creative about what you honor and how you go about it. Lola broke up with a long-term live-in and sent out invitations: "It's my party and I'll cry if I want to." The guests wore black. They listened to sad love songs and lit candles. Celebrations don't always need to be full of frivolity. It's the acknowledgment of what we're going through that make them meaningful.

As children we were enchanted with traditions—from candles on a birthday cake to Easter-egg hunts. Commemorating holidays delighted us and we looked forward to them. We may have grown up, but we still need rituals to draw us together and give us a sense of belonging. You don't have to be part of a couple to thrive on traditions. Lydia takes her single girlfriends for a sunrise picnic each summer. When one of the friends got

> As children we were enchanted with traditions—from candles on a birthday cake to Easter-egg hunts.

married, Lydia kept the picnic for singles only. "The picnic is really more than a picnic," she told me. "It started because I wanted to share the sunrise with someone special. My boyfriend and I had just broken up, so I invited my girlfriends instead. I was tearful on that first picnic, but crying and sharing the sunrise with my girlfriends helped me feel like I could go on. The picnic has become a reminder for us that no matter what happens, when the sun comes up, it's a new beginning."

Singles-only events have a different emphasis than those that include couples. That's why Pat has poker night twice a year for single friends. "We talk about the crazy ups and downs of singleness and we do a little marriage bashing too. We wouldn't be able to get that all out if couples were around." Jake and his buddies go camping and fishing—no girlfriends allowed—in Montana each summer. It's become a tradition they don't want to change.

It's wonderful to have single friends to go through life with. So celebrate with them and for them. Whether you celebrate with holding hands and chocolate or your own special rewards, pay tribute to what you're going through, and don't take each other for granted.

try this

1. Hold hands more often. The next time you walk with a friend, hold hands. Reach across the table and gently take their hand in yours. Try it—it's comforting.

2. Treat your friends to a piece of really good chocolate. Go ahead and treat yourself, too.

3. Throw a yearly "Singles Only" anniversary party.
4. What was your favorite childhood festivity? Incorporate that into your life.
5. Get out your calendar, and mark the special events you want to remember in the upcoming month and year. Keep track of your single friends' birthdays, anniversaries, and difficult rites of passage. Acknowledge them in your own distinct way. Celebrate everything!

> All I really need is love, but a little chocolate now and then doesn't hurt!
> —LUCY OF *PEANUTS* FAME, BY CHARLES M. SCHULZ

Just Friends

We'll all felt it. You meet a stranger, and instantly you're drawn to one another. There's a connection. It's as if a magnetic force is roused between you, comparable to a radio frequency—like you've been assigned a wavelength from the day you met, and you're tuned to the frequency on which the other is broadcasting. That's the way it was at first for Julia and Nichols. It was the glue that kept them together while they went through seismic adjustments figuring out how they fit in each other's lives.

By the time they met, they'd both learned that lust is not the only thing of value between a man and woman. There are many other pleasures to be enjoyed.

Nichols was comfortable around Julia; she made him laugh. Julia taught Nichols how to cook salmon and bake lemon tarts; he helped her paint her kitchen. He called her every morning to wish her a good day. They were perfect for each other, but not in the way we often think when we think of a man and a woman.

Is there such a thing as platonic love? Does every male/female relationship turn into romance? It can be difficult to distinguish between sexual, romantic, and friendly feelings.

> **Is there such a thing as platonic love? Does every male/female relationship turn into romance?**

It takes lots of communicating about needs and expectations to figure it out. Sexual tension may be present too, but it's not always wise to act on. That's what Julia and Nichols decided. You see, Nichols was sexually attracted to shy skinny girls; Julia was fluffy. Julia liked men with jingle in their pockets. Nichols was flat broke—he didn't own a television, had no fancy clothes, no health insurance, and no car. He hitched a ride, rode the bus, walked, ran, or bicycled wherever he went. He was always late. That bugged Julia. He had his shortcomings, but he was sweet and funny. They laughed at the same jokes. He held her hand, and he mowed her lawn. It was hard for him to pay attention, but when he did, he said the sweetest things. "You're alive, Julia, that's what I like about you; you're warm and enthusiastic." He called her "Honey." He didn't hold a grudge, and she liked that.

They were friends. Affectionate, for sure, but not sexual. They were platonic companions. They watched over each other. They were there for each other, and that's the way they wanted it. When she didn't have a date, he escorted her to parties and flirted with her girlfriends. Julia and Nichols cared for each other deeply, but they were not in love. They opted for friendship. If they had jumped into the sack, they might have tried to change each other. He said, and she agreed, "It's a small intersection where we meet, but there's so much tenderness there."

Men and women are not always on the road to romance, but cultural images are hard to overcome. In the past people rarely formed friendships with the opposite sex—they were off limits to each other except as marriage partners. Fortunately, we're moving beyond that now. Romance is not the only prototype for a relationship between men and women. There's also deep affection that comes through sharing common interests. A friend who makes you laugh is a treasure. The qualities you can tolerate in a friendship you may not be able to tolerate in a romantically committed love affair. Some people are drawn to each other, but that doesn't mean they can live together.

> The qualities you can tolerate in a friendship you may not be able to tolerate in a romantically committed love affair.

If you like the opposite-sex perspective, perhaps you might consider choosing friendship instead of romance. There are benefits in forming those alliances. Women spend the majority of their time together discussing their feelings, while men tend to be action oriented. Men play and watch sports. Rarely do they share feelings or personal reflections with each other. Opposite-sex camaraderie adds variety and sparkle.

"Are you really just friends?" people often asked Julia and Nichols.

"We're not destined for romance," they answer. "We like each other too much to go there," they laugh. "We're too friendly for that."

try this

1. Appreciate the pleasures of platonic love. Not everyone has to fit in a romantic box. Tell the person, "I hope we can be friends."

2. Use friend-bonding activities to get the friendship rolling. Invite him or her to join you in a group activity. Go bowling, line dancing, play volleyball. Confide in the person that you would like to be friends.

3. If you decide to pass on lust for the sake of an enduring friendship, communicate about your needs and expectations. That's the key to the success in coed friendships. Tell the person what you appreciate about him or her.

4. If you want to meet men, get involved in coed sports. If you want to meet women, go dancing.

5. Stretch beyond the romantic box. Just because a person isn't marriage material that doesn't mean you can't be close friends. Friendship is the relationship we all need to help us through all our other relationships.

If you want to sacrifice the admiration of many men for the criticism of one, go ahead, get married.

—KATHARINE HEPBURN

So Many Fish

According the U.S. Census Bureau, between 1970 and 1996, the number of women living alone doubled to 14.6 million. The number nearly tripled for men, jumping from 3.5 million to 10.3 million. That's a lot of fish!

However, just because there are a lot of fish, that doesn't mean you'll catch one—at least not every time you go fishing. My friend Sam has taught me a lot about the art of sport fishing and a little about men, and I think it's advice we can all learn from. Fishing is not a science (neither are men or women). Just because you cast your line doesn't guarantee that a fish will bite. Catching fish is not entirely in the fisherman's control. The question of whether you reel one in depends on many variables— the weather, the bait, and if the fish are hungry. Even expert fishermen equipped with all the latest gear might spend a whole season and barely get a nibble.

A genuine fisherman (or woman) takes pleasure from wading in the water, lounging in the boat, and bragging about the big one that got away. They enjoy the casting as much as the catching. A true fisherman wouldn't consider giving up the sport just because he didn't land a fish. He knows that sooner or later he'll get one, no need to worry about that. Fishing is just as much about breathing fresh air, swatting mosquitoes, and telling fish stories as it is about catching fish. No one's keeping score. The pleasure doesn't depend on the outcome. It doesn't hinge on how many fish are in the bucket; instead, it depends on the person doing the fishing. The joy springs from the heart of the fisherman.

Sam's an avid fisherman. He likes hooking up his boat the night before, waking up early, putting on his fishing vest and cap, and being on the lake as the sun comes up. He likes the fog and the cool breeze on his skin. He likes drinking a beer while he's waiting. He takes his grandson fishing. Sometimes Josh catches the only fish, but Sam doesn't mind. "It was his turn," Sam says, "I've caught plenty." That's the way it is with men and women, dating and mating. Everyone seems to get a turn. It's the ones who don't learn the art that forgo the pleasure.

Now I may not care that much about fishing, but I do like Sam (and men). I like his energy, and he has taught me a few things. "You can't learn fishing from a book, you've got to get out and do it," he says. "Good casting is about timing." He tells me stories about the lake, the birds, and the bait. He taught me about percentages and odds.

When singles hear those statistics about getting older and having fewer opportunities, we get discouraged. Those horrible statistics about the ratio of men to women make you feel as if you're standing in a room with the 14 million single women and 10 million single men and like you'll never get another turn. "Statistics," Sam says, "are good for mergers and buying real estate, but not for fishing. Forget percentages," he advises. "Go where the fish go, and go where the fewest fishermen go."

Whether it's fishing or finding someone to click with, Sam is right. Statistics have nothing to do with it. Connecting with a man or a woman, like fishing, belongs to another realm—the realm of the miraculous, where business strategies and statistics don't apply.

A wonderful life doesn't hinge on whether or not you have a mate; it depends on your attitude toward what's possible. The wonderful thing about being single is that you can hang out with lots of different characters who know all kinds of stuff—from fishing, to statistics, to dancing. When you're a couple, you're sorta stuck learning only from each other.

> A wonderful life doesn't hinge on whether or not you have a mate; it depends on your attitude toward what's possible.

try this

1. If you want to date, you can, but you have to go out and participate in something.
2. Apply Sam's fishing guidelines: "Go where the fish go, and go where the fewest fishermen go."
3. Show up, participate, and eventually you'll get your turn.
4. If you want to meet men, take up fishing; if you want to meet women, go dancing.
5. Join a writer's group, and write about "The one that got away." If you work hard enough at writing, you might get your story published, see your name in print, and who knows where that might lead!

I wasn't young, I wasn't pretty, it was necessary to find other weapons.

—DOMINIQUE AURY

Looking-for-a-Lover Burnout

Looking for a lover is tiring. It's exhausting! It wears you out! Everywhere you go you're looking, sizing people up, searching, hoping. In the grocery store, at the mall, at the juice bar, on the tennis court. It's enough to send you right over the edge. You're looking, but pretending that you're not looking.

It's perfectly normal to want a special someone, but frequently, in the quest to find that person, we may suffer from Looking-for-a-Lover Burnout syndrome.

Burnout happens when we've been looking and looking and going to all the right places (for months and even years), but even after all that effort, all that doing, nothing truly satisfying has happened. We bravely go to dance after dance, we go to hear this lecture and that lecture, and though we may have had zillions of dates, we're practically right where we started. We've talked to umpteen candidates and heard their life stories. We've memorized countless names, and written down oh so many phone numbers.

It happens to all of us. We grow weary, heartsick, and tired of looking. When that happens, the quickest, easiest cure is simply to stop for a while. Replace looking for someone with doing something, doing something that comforts our soul.

When Selma is tortured by wanting a new lover, she paints. "I paint and I paint and I paint. I can't fall in love just because I want to, but I can paint." Selma disappears for weekends, absorbed in shapes and colors, brushes, and ceiling-high canvases. "Sensuous textures and vibrant colors consume me. Eight hours can pass without my once ruminating over lovers. It's magnificent."

Robert hasn't been involved with anyone for several years and cheerfully tells his friends, "I'm seeing my glider," when they ask him about it. He built it in his barn. It wasn't that he intended to get so involved—it just happened. "It's like I'm taken over and I forget all about other lovers when I'm with *My Girl* (the name of his plane). Although she's definitely more expensive than my last wife."

Dylan didn't have much success finding lovers, so he stopped pursuing women and began studying them. He took a class on women's literature and studied women in film. He listened to what women talk about to find out what women want. It helped a lot because eventually a woman found him.

Creativity heals your broken heart and takes you to a place inside your soul that you may have forgotten. "My piano compositions," Riley says, "were at their most melodious when I was living alone in Atlanta, before I had any boyfriends."

Just because we don't have a lover right now, that doesn't mean we never will again. Lovers are luxuries, but creativity— well, that's an absolute necessity. It keeps the juices flowing. Such playful acts keep us carefree until our next admirers show up.

try this

1. When you're suffering from Looking-for-a-Lover Burnout, stop looking, and immerse yourself in a creative pursuit.
2. Study the opposite sex (or the same sex, if that's what you're into). Take a class about women's issues. Find out what interests men by hanging out with the men you already know.

3. Commit to being a live wire! Add artistic flair to your clothes, your home, and your attitude.
4. Imagine living juicy, walking juicy, talking juicy.
5. Designate one day a month as a "no rush" day. It's amazing what happens when you slow down and don't push.

> I'm not single, I'm busy.
>
> —RENE ZELLWEGER

What Are You Waiting For?

Hannah has a unique hobby. She spends hours in the dark-room, developing and enlarging prints. Then she writes anec-dotes, poetry, and stories and combines them all with images into a one-of-a-kind coffee-table scrapbook, which she has enti-tled *Men I Have Known and Loved.* Her one and only book begins with a poem dedicated to her first love—Dad. Glimpses of men—some who've stayed, some who've come and gone—are displayed throughout the pages. There are two grandpas, her older brother, and the next-door neighbor she had a crush on since she was eleven. Her first date from junior high, the long-haired counselor from summer camp, her prom date, three college sweethearts, the guys from Europe, the guy in jeans, the one-night stand, the tennis pro, and the biceps of her trainer.

Unlike Hannah, Sara is still waiting to dive into her passion. She wants a garden but never plants one. She dreams of tomatoes and lettuce, sunflowers and edible flowers. She sits for hours at the library reading gardening books and designing elaborate borders. Still, she never plants a seed. She justifies her decision saying,

"I'd rather have someone to share it with." She gives hundreds of "I'd like to, but . . ." excuses. "I'll wait," she says, "until I have a permanent home and someone to share it with." Sara prides herself on her patience, but when spring comes, she's melancholy.

Will could show Sara another way. Will grows tomato plants on his windowsill and cultivates the yard for a tiny pea patch. I asked him, "Why are you planting a garden when you're leaving on sabbatical next week?" He said, "I like gardens. I plant them even if I'm not around to see them bloom."

Twenty-seven-year-old Ivan is short and mopey. He works as an accountant. He talks slow and moves slow. He complains, "It never works out with women." He doesn't know why. He gripes, "Women don't like short men." He's convinced that his height is the reason it never works out. He wants a woman so badly that almost any woman will do. "What do you do when you're not working?' I ask him. "Nothing," he answers. "What excites you?" I ask. "Nothing much," he answers.

Twenty-six-year-old Joel is short, and everyone agrees he dates "hot" girls. I ask him how he does it. "If you talk with girls about what it is that excites you, if you talk about yourself and your passion, they like it."

Connor, Dylan, and Aaron, all great guys in their thirties, huddle together and complain that all the best girls are taken. Even when they're sitting in the middle of a crowded club, surrounded by lots of women, they moan about not being able to hook up. They're very good at complaining, but they're not good at taking any action. They don't move from their seats. They don't talk to any women—they make assumptions and that's as far as it goes.

We've all done it. Put our passions on the back burner, complained that all the good ones are taken, and made assumptions. What are we waiting for? There are literally hundreds of things to do and hundreds of people to meet. People who, like us, are yearning to share a moment of interaction and yearning to meet a new person.

To make anything happen, we have to make the effort, whether it's taking pictures, planting a garden, or meeting a new person. We have to smile and look interested. We have to get off the couch and get moving. We have to say the first word and be friendly. We can make a choice to stay in or go out. We can shop at the same supermarket or we can go across town to a little deli. We can sign up for a class or watch television. We can stare at the ground and be disinterested or we can make eye contact and say good morning. We can wait for the right moment to come along, or we can seize the moment and get started.

> **What are we waiting for? To make anything happen, we have to make the effort.**

try this

1. Jump into your passion. Focus on what it is that tickles your fancy, arouses enthusiasm, lights your fire, fuels your dreams.

2. Design your own coffee-table book and fill it with passionate color, words, and pictures.

3. Ask yourself, "What am I waiting for?" And then remind yourself that if you're constantly waiting for the right moment, nothing will ever happen.

4. Learn Italian. Rent a villa in Italy and converse with the locals. If you don't want to do that, then do something else, but get off your duff and get going.

5. Don't fill up your life looking for someone to love. Show by what you're doing that you are somebody to love.

> Be daring, be different, be impractical. Be anything that will assert imaginative vision against the play-it-safers, the creatures of the common place, the slaves of the ordinary.
>
> —Sir Cecil Beaton

Peek into the Future

"I worry that I'll be single forever," thirty-year-old Meg told me. "Does what you worry about always come true?" I asked. "No," she answered. "You'd like to be married?" I asked. "I haven't met the right guy yet," she answered, "but when I do, I want to be ready." "In my experience," I said, "that's the perfect approach." Believe that what you want is coming, and get ready.

I can't predict the future, and you probably can't either, but it's hard to change our habit of future-tripping. So I've developed a technique that you might find useful. Suppose for a moment that you could gaze into a crystal ball. Suppose that you discovered that you would be single for the rest of your life, that you'll never have another relationship. What would you do? Is there anything that you'd do differently?

You can learn about yourself by answering that question, and you can learn a lot about other singles by asking them. I asked Andrea, and she said, "I'd stop putting any energy into thinking about a relationship, planning, waiting or looking. I'd try harder to find fulfillment in the things I already do." Andrea was surprised by her own answer. She thought about it for a moment and could see that she wasn't putting her full energy into her own satisfaction.

Here's a sample of other answers to my crystal ball survey:

- "I would accept it. I wouldn't do anything differently. I don't feel tied to a specific vision for my life." —A twenty-five-year-old woman
- "I'd stay in really good shape so that I could always attract women." —A twenty-five-year-old man
- "I'd be sad. I'd shed tears, and then I'd continue to treat myself very well." —A thirty-year-old woman
- "I can't imagine that. I'd just keep right on doing what I'm doing." —A forty-year-old man
- "I would never say never, but I'll be all right if I don't. I might have some sadness about it at first and I'd shed some tears, but I would go about treating myself well, enjoying my friends, buying myself roses, going to the spa, eating scrumptious dinners out in my great neighborhood, and taking weekend trips." —A fifty-year-old woman
- "I'd continue doing what I'm doing right now, making my life as good as possible. In fact, that's the best way to prepare. The more you seek a lover, the less chance you have to get one. The more happy you are with yourself, the more likely people will want to be with you." —A sixty-year-old man

- "I've never expected to have another relationship, and I'm always surprised when I do." —A seventy-six-year-old woman

I ask the crystal-ball question of myself on New Year's Eve, as a way of taking a personal inventory, and it's better than resolutions. It reminds me not to worry about looking for a soul mate but rather to pour my total energy into making myself happy.

We can't predict the future, the what, the how, or the when, but we can enjoy what's happening right now. When something happens in our lives, we can label it "good" or "awful." We can say, "It's awful to be single," or we can say, "It's good to be single." We can say, "Right now it's good to be single." In my experience, the more we say, "Right now it's good to be single," the happier we are and the brighter our future is.

> The more we say, "Right now it's good to be single," the brighter our future is.

try this

1. Choose a "That's good" attitude. Say, "It's good to be single," or "Right now, it's good to be single."
2. Conduct your own crystal ball survey on yourself and those around you.
3. Break your habit of future-tripping. Forget all about "Will I Be Single Forever?" Don't even think it—it makes everything very weird and tense when you think in terms of "forever."

4. Put a rubber band around your wrist, and every time you think about the future, pull the band gently. Say, "Right now, it's good to be single."

5. Practice an attitude of gratitude. Say out loud, "Good things are here," and name them.

If you're saddled by the need to know the outcome before you set out, you limit your possibilities.

—JANET CARLSON FREED

Looking Good

Here's a fantastic exercise
that will allow you to see
yourself with new appreciation.
It's called the mirror meditation
And this is how it's done.

At the same time each day,
Dim the lights, light a candle, and play soothing music.
Wrap yourself in a cozy blanket,
Sit in front of a full-length mirror, and
Gaze directly into your reflection.
Allow your thoughts to come and go.
At the end of twenty minutes
Write down what you saw.
Do this for five consecutive days.

6

You're Going to Make It After All

A single life is about growth and movement. It's a soulful, holy walk, an evolution of the soul, a glorious rite of passage. Singles are everywhere. We live in a time of possibilities. We're free to explore our individuality and find creative ways to open our hearts and love. The "stuff of life" is right smack in the middle of every day. We've come a long way. Not only has the single stigma vanished—we're living longer, and being single is a significant stage in adult development. It's a magical transition to go from feeling sad and single to feeling thrilled to be alive; to arrive at the place of knowing that our one single human life is not irrelevant, that our life has meaning and purpose and we are delighted to handle it.

Ah, This!

There are notable passages in the life of a single adult. In our journey from single, to partnered, to single, and back again, we uncover the sections of our being that need attention. We all have holes in our being, and we try to fill those holes with a significant other. But when the other person disappears, those holes are back again, leaving us feeling open and vulnerable.

If, as adults, we are to become whole, our glorious assignment is to treasure the single segment that we are in. To achieve wholeness, first we have to experience the void, the hole, the missing component. We have to hang in there, lean into the hollow, explore the unfilled slots. We have to heal our wounds, go into this emptiness,

> To achieve wholeness, first we have to experience the void.

allow the absence, and watch. We have to be with ourselves while we long for the other.

Mastering singleness is sometimes a slow and thoughtful process. It requires contemplation. Our lives are no one's responsibility but our own. There are many things that we have no control over, and those things we are not responsible for. But we are responsible for how we respond to our own circumstances. Dwelling on the past won't undo what is already gone, and fretting about the future won't change what's coming.

> Dwelling on the past won't undo what is already gone, and fretting about the future won't change what's coming.

By letting go of fixed goals, fixed ideas, tensions, fears, opinions, and judgments, as well as the habit of analyzing, of explaining everything, of making excuses, and of thinking we know best, we can live a wonderful single life. We don't have to be in a relationship to be content. We're not insignificant if we don't have a significant other. We can be great without a great lover, boyfriend, girlfriend, partner, or spouse.

When we let go of seeking a relationship; when we let go of complaining that all the good ones are taken; when we let go of scanning the room to see if anyone is our type; when we let go of feeling unlovable because there's no lover in sight; when we let go of talking endlessly about it, we can partake fully in all our blessings. We're not lost in thought, not anticipating this or that. We're not lost in some abstraction; we're right here in the now, fully alert, and present—which feels great in and of itself! Then we can smell the coffee, the fresh air, and the roses. Then we can talk with the people we meet and be glad to know them. It's in that "Ah, this!" moment, with all our mental gibberish out of the way, that we're fully primed for a fantastic life.

We live in a magical world. Yet so often we don't enjoy those sweet moments that make life so special. The more we understand the nature of our temporary life, the more full of wonder we are. When we love without demanding, when we love without grasping, we've ripened. Then we can relax and celebrate, love, and do great things.

try this

1. Blow soap bubbles and watch them float by. Let the fragile bubbles remind you that life is momentary and slipping by.

2. Practice loving. Be a love bug for a day. Say thank you to the bus driver; open the door for ladies; be gentle with the clerk; be generous with praise.

3. Pause and reflect. Connect to the mystery by praying, by singing, by dancing, by sitting silently and giving thanks.

4. Draw a picture with chalk on the sidewalk; draw a heart in the sand; plant flowers along the roadside; say hello to and pet a dog.

5. Show appreciation toward yourself, too. Write a secret list of what you've overcome. You don't need to brag about it, because it shows. Just take a moment to acknowledge it for yourself.

Enroll in Laughing School

It was a magazine article that triggered my hiccup sobs and sidesplitting laughter. There it was, on the cover of a women's magazine, in bold red letters: "The Chances of a Thirty-Five-Year-Old Woman of Finding a Husband, see page 67." Doomed by the distinction of carrying every marital status there was, I was eager for advice. Turning to page sixty-seven, I read the sobering details persuading me that at my advanced age of thirty-four-and-a-half, I had a better chance of meeting a movie star, like Johnny Depp or George Clooney, than I did of finding a husband.

The statistics attested to a grim reality: I was no longer wife material! And if that wasn't enough, I was broke. I couldn't even pay the electric bill, let alone travel. Which meant that the possibility of getting out of the suburbs and encountering a movie star were beyond my reach. No doubt about it—I was rejected, dejected, a hopeless case, stuck in the suburbs, alone and lonely, no husband, no white picket fence, no movie stars, no prospects.

My existential crisis came tumbling down upon me like water over Niagara Falls that very afternoon. It had been years since I'd cried. I didn't cry at Jack's funeral because Jacqueline Kennedy hadn't cried at her husband's funeral. I had no other role models. I didn't know any young widows, so like Jackie before me, I remained composed. I followed Jack's casket down the center aisle, sat motionless during the proper Catholic funeral, and closed my eyes as the casket was lowered into the ground. What good would it do to wail or moan, to

> **What good would it do to wail or moan, to feel sorry for myself? It wouldn't bring my husband back.**

feel sorry for myself? It wouldn't bring my husband back.

The day I married my second husband, I downed a bottle of champagne instead of crying. I didn't cry when he had an affair with a friend or when he couldn't be reached the night Amanda was born. I gave in when he pleaded and begged for forgiveness. I cried on the inside and suffered with migraines.

But with that crazy article came my epiphany. Before I'd finished reading, I was sobbing. I was powerless over my tears. I couldn't hold them back. I couldn't contain the lump in my throat, couldn't stop my body from shaking. I could no longer repress my grief. The pain I'd stored away over the years erupted from my belly. I may have convinced family and friends that I was fine, but I could no longer deceive myself. I was devastated.

I knew that life was difficult and unfair. I'd read numerous stories of movie stars, sports heroes, and politicians who had every advantage—wealth and fame—yet remained morally bankrupt and discontent. I even knew a few pillars of the community who didn't deserve their good fortune. I also knew of people who had nothing but deserved much more.

People everywhere suffer injustices. It was the reason I'd gone into social work in the first place, to fight the wrongs and make a difference. I'd believed, as Jack had, that people could with a helping hand pull themselves out of the muck. After all, he certainly had. I believed it wholeheartedly, but I never thought I'd be so low. I'd been smug not noticing that I myself might need a helping hand.

That afternoon, on my knees, I wept for myself, for Jack, for sweet Amanda, for the condition of the world. Once I worked placing kids in foster homes; now I felt displaced myself. I cried for the boat people, the homeless, the sick, the unappreciated, the misunderstood. I knew that there were people worse off than I was, but at that moment I was connected in spirit with the most distraught. I missed Jack, missed being his wife. I wanted my old life back. I cried so hard I couldn't speak or even catch my breath. I remembered Jack blowing me a kiss as he was led away through the double doors of the emergency room. "Don't worry," he said, "It's only an upset stomach." Was he scared? Why did Jack die so young? Was it fate? Was there a higher purpose? If God is in charge, why is there so much suffering? If this is godly design, where is the good?

> I remembered Jack blowing me a kiss as he was led away through the double doors of the emergency room.

My sobbing lament reached such a feverish complaint that it startled me. I couldn't remember ever making that much noise. It wasn't my style to throw temper tantrums, make scenes, or place demands. But I didn't know how else to gain God's attention. I was tired of being a good little girl, tired of being ignored. I wanted God and all the saints in Heaven—if there were any—to come to my rescue. My screeching caught me off guard, surprised me, woke me up. For a moment, something inside me shifted. It was as if I'd been in a trance. Once a passive participant letting life happen, now I was suddenly awake and alert. I became tuned in to a realm of silence residing within. Deep within my soul—at least I thought it was my soul—there wasn't a ripple of disturbance. It was as if I'd become an impartial observer. A witness to my own suffering, I was able to watch my tears and sorrow yet no longer was troubled by them. I thought it odd. Perhaps I'd gone mad, but it was such a relief that I laughed. And it wasn't a polite, proper Sunday-school-girl laugh but a belly laugh that shook my body and frightened five-month-old Amanda, who'd been lying on the floor, cheerfully playing with her toes.

My attention turned to little Amanda and soon we were conversing in cooing sounds. Nothing had changed really, yet everything was altered. I felt cleansed. The world simply looked fresh and full of possibilities. My focus shifted. How it had happened, I couldn't be sure. Had I undergone a spiritual transformation or merely gone over the edge? As I basked in the reprieve from my pain, I busied myself in the glory of diapering and feeding my smiling baby. I'd had a good cry, and I felt better. Was is possible that tears and laughter went together? As a child I remembered laughing, rolling on the floor with friends until tears were streaming down our faces. Now I'd cried so hard that I was laughing. Could pain and joy go hand in hand? Certainly every mother knows the excruciating pain of childbirth followed by the exalted state of bliss of greeting a new soul. I promised myself that from now on, I wouldn't hold back my tears. If I needed to cry, I would let them flow. Had I deadened myself to my pain and, as a consequence, missed the joy of being alive? I had nothing to lose by checking it out further, and for a few seconds I was excited by the possibilities.

If it's true that two people in the world can be connected by six degrees of separation, then why is it impossible for an independent woman to meet her soul mate? "It's all a cosmic joke," I thought, and laughed even louder. In fact I felt so good that I stopped thinking. My mind was clear. I got up and took Amanda for a walk.

try this

1. Don't believe the statistics about age, happiness, and being single. Don't even read them. If they didn't ask you, then they have nothing to do with you.
2. Notice that laughter and tears go together. Think about it. If you've ever laughed so hard that tears started rolling down your cheeks, if you've ever cried so long and hard that you felt relieved and started laughing, then you know for sure that they follow each other.
3. Don't squelch your tears. Cry whenever you need too. Cry loudly, freely, and hard for as long as it takes to clear your pipes and to get your funny bone going.
4. After you've had a good cry, get out of the house. Go for walks, lots of walks. Take your dog, your kids, or the neighbor.
5. Laugh and be amused at yourself. Cosmic jokes are everywhere.

You grow up the day you have your first real laugh at yourself.

—Ethel Barrymore

Go with the Wind

Katherine is a sensuous lady. She sparkles with life. She dresses in flowing silk, chenille, and velvet. She has gray hair—which she sometimes colors burgundy—and brilliant red fingernails. She lives alone in a two-story house with brightly colored walls, flowers in pots, and flouncy pillows in front of the fireplace. She's passionate, although she hasn't had a sexual encounter in more than ten years. It isn't a morality issue. It's just that, like many other confident, self-assured women, she just doesn't meet that many eligible partners. She knows women who meet men through the personals, and she's even heard of a woman who placed an ad for sex in a literary magazine and then wrote a book about her experiences. She has nothing against that—it's just that she isn't inclined to place ads. Being a passionate lady, she misses the sexual connection, but her life is full with men friends, girlfriends, family, art, and work. Occasionally she complains about the lack of sexual dalliances that she freely partook of in youth, but she's at peace now—more or less—with having that aspect of her life be finished.

Yes, you can still giggle and "get it on" at sixty.

It wasn't finished. The morning "after," she couldn't wait to telephone her girlfriends and giggle about it. Yes, you can still giggle and "get it on" at sixty.

She met Clay, she forgot to ask his last name, at a party. Nothing special, nothing notable, nothing earthshaking at first glance, except that he wore jeans and a red plaid shirt and was intriguingly rough around the edges. They sat next to each other on the couch and talked. They talked about art and browsed the hostess's book collection. They walked in the garden and smelled the herbs. They sat on the patio, smoked one cigarette, and shared a pot of tea. They swooned in the center of an energy bubble. He leaned forward and asked if she could feel the magnetic attraction between them. She could. He invited her home, she went, they kissed, they touched, they rolled around, their edges melted. They watched the sun come up, they went out to breakfast, and he drove her home. She called her friends and lolled in her overstuffed chair for the entire day.

It's a great story, a true story, but not an unusual one (except when it happens to you, course). It happens all the time, this little thing called sexual magnetism. It happens even to independent, fulfilled, sensuous, old-timers like Katherine and Clay (who, by the way, hadn't had sex in two years). Men and women who have been celibate for years can get turned on. This is even true of women like Katherine, who are so involved in life that they temporarily lose interest in sex, can and do attract men. And it's true of men like Clay, who thought they couldn't, but still could. You can be celibate for days or years. Then one night the wind can blow in another direction, and the next morning you can be dizzy, pulsating, and flying high.

> You can be celibate for days or years. Then one night the wind can blow in another direction, and the next morning you wake up dizzy, pulsating, and flying high.

To go with the wind, you have to be willing to take a chance, to jump, to leap, to risk. You have to disrobe and stand naked in all your innocent loveliness. You have to fight that powerful urge to turn and run away, to pretend that you don't care and don't notice. You have to fight that tendency to be above it all. You have to be willing, willing to want it and go for it. You have to drop your fears about your body and let go of your judgments about right and wrong. Self-criticism and thoughts of right and wrong don't mix well with sexual magnetism. Instead, such thoughts diminish sexual pleasure.

Sexuality and sensuality are not things you can force. Rather, you have to become receptive to them. Good sex depends less on beauty, less on technique, less on age, less on tight muscles, and more on how appreciative you are. And to be really appreciative means that you are content, content and thrilled to be alive with your juices flowing.

try this

1. Become receptive to and enjoy your sensuous nature. Dress sensuously. Let yourself feel sexual.
2. Take it slow. Don't hide or run away. Having sexual feelings does not have to lead to the expression of sexual feelings. And the expression of sexual feelings does not have to lead to sexual activity. Each stage can be enjoyed in and of and for itself.
3. Develop the ability to look another person in the eye. Not harshly or menacingly, but softly, with wide-eyed wonder.

That sweet little skill is tremendously effective in enhancing one's capacity for love play.

4. If you want something that will attract people to you, try genuinely raising your self-esteem. Ask yourself, "What is one thing that I can do that would raise my self-esteem?" Do that thing. It's the secret charm that works wonders.

5. Be turned on to life. Listening to music, let the music vibrate the pores of your skin. Washing dishes, let the suds bathe your hands. Walking the dog, enjoy being pulled. Enjoy the leisureliness of a stroll, or the sweat of jogging, or the tang of a breeze.

> Ultimately, there are only two reasons to resist temptation: that you like your life that way it already is, and that you're extremely tired.
>
> —WILLIAM ASHOKA ROSS

Indulge Your Whims

Ella is in a single phase and happily on her own. She likes her studio apartment and her morning schedule. Her clothes are clean, ironed, and hanging in the closet, ready for her at a moment's notice. She runs nearly every day and cooks a delicious dinner for herself every night with food that she buys from the farmer's market. She loves her daily routine; it's her companion, her comfort. She pays attention to the fine points, the small details, and by doing this, she feels nurtured.

She walks to work and says hello to people she passes. She discovered the best bakery for an afternoon chocolate chip–

cookie break; she's learning how to knit from a neighbor and tiling a table in red mosaic. Since Ella doesn't have a romance vying for her attention, she's taking good care of herself, indulging her whims, and smiling.

Ella's friends Solomon and Bernie are in the falling-in-love phase and are consumed with their new girlfriends. Ella's girlfriend Phoebe has a new romance, too. They're all giddy, dizzy, and disoriented. Giddy from gazing into each other's eyes, dizzy with the flush of desire, and disoriented because relationship management takes up so much time. Phoebe and her guy talk on the phone all night. She likes it, but she's too tired for morning yoga and hasn't seen her best friend, Ella, in weeks. It's the same for Solomon. He's devoting all his energy to his new girlfriend, Leila, and hasn't done his laundry. Bernie's in the same predicament. He hasn't seen his friends enough either because he and Abbey have an unspoken commitment for Friday nights. He's gained five pounds because they eat out so much.

Sure, each of these couples likes falling asleep with their limbs tangled, but the initial intoxication of romance is beginning to wear off and they're pining for a bit of individuality. "I need alone time," they all agree. Ella listens to all of their stories. Bernie tells her, "My day is consumed navigating around Abbey."

When Phoebe and Ella finally have a chance to catch up, Ella hears the same story: "I need a night alone to do my nails and clean my apartment."

Solomon tells Ella, "I can't find half my wardrobe because I've left it at Leila's house; it's disorienting." Solomon complains that he hasn't been playing his guitar like he used to do almost every day, "When I think of myself and who I am, I think I'm a musician. That's my identity, but lately I'm not a musician at all, I'm just a lover boy!"

"I was alone for so long that I'm enjoying being in a relationship," Bernie says, "but there are some things that you can't do when you have another person to think about. When you're alone you can change your plans on a whim or you can really get into your routine."

Phoebe agrees, "When you're putting your energy into another person, you don't have time for daily details and I miss those things."

Ella listens to her friends' frustrations, offering encouragement and advice. "You'll figure out the right balance," she says. "Enjoy this phase. It will get easier, you'll see."

As she offers her advice, Ella is tickled. She feels liberated and free. She doesn't envy her friends. She has no love jealousy, which is not easy. She doesn't have a twinge of "I wish I had a lover," because she's not deprived at all. How wonderful! Ella expects that she'll have a romance again, but right now she's indulging her whims and that fills her up.

If there's a moral of the story, it's this: Whether you're single or in a romance, individuality is a basic ingredient for happiness. Indulging your whims is a pleasure, a necessity that promotes smiling.

try this

1. When friends complain about relationship management, reassure them as gently as you can. This is not the time to brag about the perks of being single.

2. Don't be dissuaded—by your parents, your friends, or the pious—from indulging your whims, whether it's as simple as a midnight snack or as extravagant as a new car.

3. Decorate your place in accordance with your whims.

4. Bask in the pleasures of comforting details, morning routines, and spiffy clean clothes.

5. Remember, it is perfectly okay to be smug about being happy with yourself.

Find what you need, not what everyone else wants for you.

—SALMA HAYEK

Go, Get Out of Town

If life's a school, then singleness is a significant part of the curriculum. Michael's teacher for the "Traveling Solo" course was his seventeen-year-old daughter, Lila. She was his inspiration.

Since Michael's wife died, his complete and total attention had been on raising his son and daughter. Like other single parents, he absorbed himself in homework, housework, kids, and family. For years, Michael's days began before sunrise and ended at midnight, when he plopped into bed. On weekends he drove the kids to their events and caught up with laundry, the yard, and groceries. He didn't miss a personal social life. He was head of the family, and that was enough. It wasn't a sacrifice; it was what he did. Over the years, it brought him tremendous joy. On vacations he took the kids camping, and over the summers they hiked eighteen national parks. He liked hiking. It was his dream to someday go trekking in Nepal, but he doubted that he'd actually do it. His son, a college freshman, had an internship lined up for the summer. Lila was graduating from high school and would be going away to college in the fall. The kids were thriving, busy, and branching out.

Whenever he thought about traveling alone, Michael felt homesick. So instead of figuring out how to do it, he put Nepal on the back burner. "When the kids are through with college, we'll go together," he told himself. At least that's what he thought he'd do, until Lila expanded his vision. Her guts spurred him to push beyond his imaginary limits. Here's what happened.

The night before Lila's senior prom, her date abruptly backed out. The reasons that he canceled aren't important, but the way she handled the disappointment is. When Lila's date told her that he wouldn't be taking her to the prom, she laid down on her bed and cried hard for about fifteen minutes. Then she took a shower. Michael paced from room to room, resisting his urge to strangle the guy. Michael offered to fly Lila's brother home to be her escort, but Lila said it wasn't necessary. Michael threatened to call the guy's parents, which Lila wouldn't hear of. "We'll start a new tradition, called 'Father-Daughter go to the Prom,'" he offered. Lila refused that too. "I'm going alone! I'm taking myself to the prom." And that's exactly what she did. She went to her senior prom without a date.

The day of the prom, just as she had planned, she met up with girlfriends at the mall for hair and makeup. Her friends and their dates invited her to join them for dinner, but Lila decided to have Dad and her grandparents take her out. After dinner she came home, put on her long pink dress and matching sandals, and had Dad drive her to the prom. She stepped out of the car and went to the dance alone!

A prom is a rite of passage, and this was one for Michael, too. "If she can go to the prom alone, I can go to Nepal alone."

The kids went off to college, and Michael booked his trip. It was the first time that he'd ever traveled without a companion. Sure, it made him nervous to think about not having anyone to share his impressions with, and sure he felt a pit in his stomach not seeing a familiar face in a strange land. But every time he thought about backing out, Lila's prom spurred him on.

A first-time solo trip is more than a vacation. It's about more than sightseeing or being a tourist. It's an expedition of gumption, a rite of passage in self-reliance. There's a quality of seeking and searching in those inaugural ventures. Even if the first solo jaunt only takes you a hundred miles away, going alone is going away in order to find out something about yourself that you couldn't have found out at home. It's liberating! Your senses come alive, and you're alert. Packing a suitcase and heading out gives you roaming space and roving options. You're no longer slowed by cold feet. You're moving. You've got choices. You're not constrained by the whims of a companion; you can head out in your own direction.

try this

1. Plan an overnighter close to home to give you practice sleeping in a hotel, eating out, and exploring. Do this a couple of times, and you'll be less anxious when you're ready for uncharted territory.

2. Make an itinerary. You don't have to follow it, but it's good to have in case you have an "Oh my gosh, I'm in a strange land" freak-out moment. And it will keep you on course.

3. Pack for physical and emotional comfort. For example, pack comfy shoes and a good book. Pack an outfit that you really like and some bubble bath. Pack CDs, books on tape, and munchies.

4. Talk to strangers. Ask for directions; ask for restaurant recommendations and entertainment suggestions. Don't just stand there—say something!

5. Write the details of your excursion on postcards, and mail them to yourself. Send postcards to friends and family, too. Brag about what you're doing and seeing. Exaggerate if you must. You'll have fun reading them when you're back home.

> There is nothing like returning to a place that remains unchanged to find the ways in which you yourself have altered.
>
> —NELSON MANDELA

I'm an Optimist, I Can't Help It!

My friend Clinton says, "If another good thing happens to me, I'll scream." He expects things to go well, and they do most of the time. He told me, "When I'm standing in a room with the door shut, the lights off, I don't feel alone. When I'm standing by a river and I can't see or hear another soul, I'm not alone, I can hear the water moving and I'm connected." That's optimism!

Twenty-seven-year-old Claire felt honored and slightly left out—even though she wasn't—being maid of honor twice in one month. Her two closest friends both got married in August. She was a pivotal part of each ceremony. She spoke at two receptions and caught two bridal bouquets. "Claire," the guests asked over and over until it got a little tiresome, "When are you getting married?" Claire, ever the optimist, replied, "I don't know, but it looks like it'll be twice."

> **Optimism is the flicker of hope underneath layers of agony and self-doubt.**

Optimism is the flicker of hope underneath layers of agony and self-doubt. It's the energy that propels us forward. Optimism is really quite sensuous. Living optimistically refreshes your body and rejuvenates your spirit. Sensuousness leads you from your restless, random obsessive thoughts back to your skin, to your flesh, to your senses—which are the interface with the world.

Audrey is a sensuous lady. She married four times and divorced four times and told her hairdresser, "I'm trying to learn from the younger generation to live together instead of tying the knot." She likes being married, and she likes being single. She likes being single more when she's married; she likes marriage more when she's single. "It's beginning to sink in," she laughs, "that alone doesn't mean lonely and together doesn't mean happy."

According to Audrey, "When I'm in one of my pessimistic moods, I take a bubble bath, put on my silk robe and get under satin sheets. In the morning I'm better, and if I'm not, I take another bath."

We're all on a road traveling to somewhere, and we all have some sense of what we're moving toward. We have an idea of where we'd like to go, but sometimes we get so afraid that we think we'll never make it. I know singles who hope they'll find a beautiful lover, but they're afraid they won't. I know singles who want to change careers, but they're afraid that it is too late, so they don't even try. Their fears take hold of them and smother their hopes. Our hope for happiness gets dampened by our fears. Our optimism is crushed by our pessimism. If our fears are stronger than our optimistic expectations, we feel panicky because we're convinced we're going to be moving down instead of up. We foresee failure, yet we go on speaking the language of hope. I know singles who throw their shoulders back and talk about being winners, but on the inside, they think of themselves as losers.

Through my own experience, I have come to know that our own impression of what we're moving toward can totally make the difference between happiness and unhappiness. I have a friend who all her life has felt that she is a "bad" and unattractive person. She would like to find a lover, and now and then she tries. But she confided to me that regardless of any effort she might make, she will only become more and more lonely as time goes by. She says she knows better, but she thinks of this as a kind of punishment for not being a really "good" person—for sometimes being spiteful and angry and so on. She is unhappy because of what she feels she is moving toward. Occasionally she even feels she will end her days destitute, abandoned, uncared for—maybe even a bag lady. And this thought haunts and torments her.

What do you feel you are moving toward? Even if you feel, like my friend, that there is no hope for you, I want to tell you that it is only a belief. It's only baggage that you're carrying around with you.

Audrey isn't always optimistic. She can be quite melancholy, and she admits to dramatic leanings. When she's in a bad mood or when things go wrong, she can flounder for days or weeks trying to snap out of it. She searches for someone to understand. She smiles and pretends that it isn't so bad. But no matter how well she fakes it, she can't force herself to feel better. When her purse and credit cards were stolen, she couldn't convince herself that there was a bright side to a thief charging more than $3,000 to her account in less than an hour. It happened right after the divorce from number four, and all seemed lost. It's in those frustrating times that she heads for the Jacuzzi. Sometimes she takes three Jacuzzi baths in one day. Instead of resisting and fighting, she gives in, takes a bath, and goes to bed. When Audrey comes around, however, she's quite forgiving. "I forgive myself and my exes. We're doing the best we can. If there's reincarnation, we'll be back and do better next time."

When aloneness grabs you by the throat and chokes out all your positive intention; when the single world seems cold and heartless; when you feel like an outsider, overwhelmed, unloved, and uncared for, consider taking a bath or soaking in a hot tub. Water is healing. All life depends on it. The body is eighty-five percent water. Water is flexible—it has no form. That's its beauty. While immersed in the tub, let the warm water be a metaphor reminding you that there are many rivers of satisfaction and fulfillment to carry you. Water is always moving.

Let it soothe your aching muscles and remind you not to become stagnant. Don't get stuck in one mindset, but stay with the tide. Singleness does have its tides. Move from one thing to another, and let the river carry you.

One more thing about Audrey—she's an activist. She's involved in grassroots movements from peace campaigns to women's rights, from collecting for the food bank to raising funds for community theater. "The one thing I'm convinced of," Audrey told me, "is that one single person can make a big difference in the world."

try this

1. Sit down. Put everything else out of your mind, and make contact with the essential goodness in you—the part of you that knows deep, deep, deep down that you are a good and worthwhile person and truly deserving. And when you've done that, complete this statement: "I am moving toward _____" (fill in the blank). Do it again and again until you really feel good about yourself.

2. Give yourself a love name. When you're feeling pessimistic, say, "It will be okay, my little skookums."

3. Dress sensuously! Sleep sensually! Take a bath.

4. Think optimistically, forgive yourself, and do away with fear-based thinking. Write this down: "Life gives me a thousand chances."

5. Write this phrase down, and put it on the bathroom mirror so that you can read it every morning: "Where I have been and what I have done do not define where I can go."

The best way to cheer yourself up is to try to cheer somebody else up.

—MARK TWAIN

When Misery Rolls In, Rent a Kayak

When people ask me, "Judy, do you like being single?" I'm careful about my answer. It's really hard for people to believe that a single person could like being single. I do like it. I didn't always. I was miserable in the first fragile stages, which often seemed to last for years. After my marriages, single life took some getting used to again. I had to wrestle with it. But not only did I get used to it, I really like living alone. Still, I don't always admit it. I'm careful not to brag. Usually I say, "There are some things I like about being single and some things that I don't." Which is also true. I like having my own space and my own moods. I like the living room walls red. I like my cozy white couch and chairs. In the summer, I like sleeping outdoors on my deck and listening to music in the middle of the night. I like stocking the refrigerator with sparkling water and take-out containers from my favorite restaurants. I like riding my bicycle during the dinner hour. I like unexpected romantic encounters. I like feeling sad about not having a partner who wants to cheer me up. I like being cheerful without having to tone myself down because my partner's feeling grumpy. What it all boils down to is that I like living in sync with my own rhythm.

What I miss about living with a partner are little things like drinking tea and reading the morning paper together. I miss having one special love who is interested in what I'm doing. What scares me the most about singleness, however, is getting caught in the wheel of wishing. Wishing for someone to be with, wishing for someone I used to be with, wishing for someone I don't even know. I don't want to waste a moment wishing. I'm persistent about that. For me, wishing for who and what you don't have is misery.

In a Singles Only workshop, a participant asked me, "Are you really okay being single?" "I'm having a very good year!" I answered. "Oh!" she said, "that scares me. I don't want to get to that place. That's what I'm fighting. If I have a good year, then it will really be over for me." I remember feeling like that myself. I remember thinking I needed to fight against singleness because if I accepted it, I wouldn't do much to change it. I agree we should figure out what we want and do what is within our power to attain it. What we all want is to feel good and have a good year. We want happiness, yet we have a tendency to make ourselves miserable to get it. I don't need to be miserable to have a good year. Still, I did reassure the woman. "Not to worry," I said, "Misery has a way of rolling in, even in a good year."

A single life is a miraculous catalyst—even if you're miserable for parts of it. Be thankful for each hour of contentment. Be grateful that you can pick out the videos and skip through the scenes you don't like. When a neighbor gave me a box of chocolates, I pinched every one to find my favorites. I'm diligent about counting my blessings, even the sweet ones that are gone—Jack, Henry, Bill, Bob-a-roo.

Be overjoyed for the opportunity to know yourself. You're in charge of you. Think about it. Isn't it amazing that one single life can be so magnificent? Aren't you glad to be alive and breathing? You can do so much—talk and laugh, walk and run, fall down, get up and dance. If you win the lottery, you don't have to share it. You've got legs! And they can take you places and bring you back again. You can save your money and fly to Bali. You've got arms and hands. You can squeeze the tooth-paste wherever you like. You can hug and cuddle; you can reach out and shake hands with everyone. You can plant flowers and cook artichokes. You can share them—or not. You've got hands to clap and toes to wiggle. You can wear san-dals in the winter and no one tells you that it's too cold to go without socks. When there's a problem, you can overcome it. You can cry and feel better. If there's an obstacle, you can figure out what to do about it or you call someone to assist you. Sure, you probably can list many shortcomings, but you can rise above annoying defects. Isn't it grand?

Singleness is a blessed period in adulthood, a significant stage of human development. A chance to find what soothes you, inspires, and moves you. Singleness is many things. It's being unsure and not knowing what's next. It's finding out. And with those simple discoveries, you've become more than what you ever envisioned for yourself.

The path to happiness is always inward, a solitary pil-grimage. When you're listening to your deepest needs and responding to them, you're tapping into lasting comfort as you move toward your center.

"I know I'll make it," Martha told me. "I woke up at five on Saturday morning, rolled out of bed, filled my thermos, and headed for the water. I rented a kayak and watched the sun come up over the lake. My former lover hated getting out of bed before the sun came up."

---

try this

1. When you're feeling absolutely devastated—which occasionally you might be—look in the mirror and say to yourself: "Singleness is not going to kill me."

2. As I advised the lady in my workshop, channel misery into energy and use it on your own behalf. Any energy is better than no energy at all.

3. Turn that miserable chip on your shoulder into curiosity. Check out singles clubs, events, workshops, and activities. You don't have to join—just check it out. Pretend you're a newspaper reporter writing an article on singles. Interview the members that tickle your fancy.

4. Act "as if" you're interested in other people. Act "as if" you're having a good day. Act "as if" you have something to offer. Act "as if" you're really a prize. Even if most of the time you don't believe it, act "as if."

5. Count your blessings, all of them, including the ones that got away. If you can't remember your blessings, rent a kayak, go out on the water, and watch the sun rise.

'It's My Life!' When this is said truly and not merely in defiance, vistas open up, opportunities arise, creative potential manifest in you to an ever increasing extent.

—WILLIAM ASHOKA ROSS

We've Got a Secret!

There are many paths to enlightenment, and singleness is one of the quickest. Forget all about vipassana, yoga, tantric sex, and tai chi. The path of being single has expanded my awareness, taught me the value of surrender, and how to accept what is. I must confess a sentimental attachment to the idea of marriage, but I am no longer ruled by the desire for it. I'm sure you know by now that I never wanted to be single. At one time, singleness to me meant lonely, unlovable, loser. From this vantage point, now, I can see that I was very mistaken. I'm no longer bedazzled as I once was by white dresses and wedding marches. I'm no longer swept away by promises. I'm passionately attracted to living utterly responsible and free.

A spiritual master once advised his followers that the grass grows by itself. I know it's true because the grass in my backyard grows wildly without my attention. But it sure doesn't get mowed by itself. I have to do that. That's the way life is. Sometimes we have to let go and do nothing, and sometimes we have to roll up our sleeves, take charge, sweat, and work hard.

A single life is full of hard soul-searching. It's growth and movement. It's an opportunity to know and appreciate all that is special about ourselves. A chance to value who we are and how far we've come; to recognize our talents and gifts and put them to good use; to acknowledge our flaws and forgive ourselves for them. There's satisfaction in being comfortable with yourself. It's not bragging to admit that you're okay being who you are. Oh sure, you've got funny quirky ways, we all do. But so what? At least we no longer take ourselves so seriously.

Singleness is astounding in its transforming power. It's a precious process of shaping and reshaping, of adding spice to our character. A few minor eccentricities, a slightly offbeat manner gives us our interesting edge.

As a single individual, each of us stands face to face with wounds that shake and question our worthiness. We're afraid, and like David standing up to Goliath, we stare into the giant face of abandonment. It takes tremendous courage, faith, and commitment to stand by and for ourselves.

> **Singleness is a precious process of shaping and reshaping, of adding spice to our character.**

We cannot escape it; we are alone. We are born alone, die alone, and deep down in our souls we live alone. Even when we're together, at the core of our being, we're absolutely alone. Aloneness is not as lonely as it is deep.

Nobody's perfect. Everybody's wounded, which means that life has left its marks. We all are scarred with tattered self-esteem, torn apart by fears that try as we might we won't be loved, shamed by some imaged physical imperfection, withered with disappointments. It's in facing these scars that we discover how to listen, how to respond, how to sustain. In doing so, we're able to reach out in compassion to ourselves and others.

Healing our wounds, and becoming whole and independent, deepens our understanding about our connection with our fellow travelers and our place in the universe. During alone moments, we're more apt to turn toward the Divine through prayer and asking for guidance. By doing so, we become more tender, more forgiving, more humble, and more humane. The world needs kind, effective, grown-up individuals. The world needs grownups who have blossomed enough to speak for what's honorable and decent. The world desperately needs to unite in love, with love, for love. After all, it's love that we all are seeking.

Becoming an independent person is a process of becoming more than we were, of opening to love in forms that we may not have known before. To resist where we find ourselves is to diminish what we could become in the end. Celebrate the courage it demands, the changes it invites, the wide-open love that it brings.

The single life is at once exciting and mundane. It's wonderful, it's fine, it's blah. It's the whole shebang. For every disappointment, for all the loneliness, and struggle, there is a counterbalancing pleasure. An excellent signpost that we've grown up is when we can make ourselves happy in our own world. If someone comes along and wants to be part of it, great! And if they never come along then we're still happy. That's our secret: We let go of what we can't control; we enjoy everything else, and we're happy.

try this

1. Say this meditation out loud: "May I be happy; may I be well. May all singles be happy; may all singles be well. May all couples be happy; may all couples be well."

2. Practice, practice, practice. The more practice you have at loving yourself, the more natural it becomes.

3. Question everything you think you have to do. Don't be afraid to live an unconventional life.

4. Recite this mantra over and over: "Happily ever after begins with me." Let it replace any negative self-talk.

5. Make your bed cozy, comfy, and cushy. Get a silver tray, a long-stemmed red rose in a vase, a beautifully folded linen napkin, and have dinner in bed.

To love oneself is the beginning of a life-long romance.

—OSCAR WILDE

Here's to a Brilliant Solo Performance

Be daring, be eccentric, be *you* without apology to anyone!

Be prepared. Be generous with your time, with your talents, with your loving.

And most of all, my friend, be generous with yourself!

And as they say before the curtain goes up,

"Darling, break a leg."

About the Author

Judy Ford is a psychotherapist in private practice in Kirkland, Washington. She is the author of these books:

Wonderful Ways to Love a Child

Wonderful Ways to Love a Teen:
Even When It Seems Impossible

Wonderful Ways to Be a Family

Wonderful Ways to Be a Stepparent

Wonderful Ways to Love a Grandchild

Expecting Baby

Between Mother and Daughter

Getting over Getting Mad

For more information, visit her Web site, *www.judyford.com*.